The Kugel Story
not just noodle pudding

2

18.95

The Kugel Story
not just noodle pudding

2

A COLLECTION OF 200 TRADITIONAL JEWISH RECIPES

175 ARE KUGELS

EVERYTHING YOU ALWAYS WANTED
TO KNOW ABOUT KUGEL
BUT DIDN'T KNOW YOU WANTED TO KNOW

Nina Yellin

Smylan Reed Books

This book is available at special discounts for bulk purchases for sales promotions, premiums, fund-raising, or educational use.

Yellin, Nina
   The kugel story: not just noodle pudding 2/Nina Yellin 2nd ed.
   p.cm.
   Includes index.
   Preassigned LCCN: 93-083644.
   ISBN 0-9622811-1-5

1. Cookery, Jewish. 2. Noodles   I.Title.

TX724.Y45 1993   641.5'676
                               QB193-348

Edited by: Cantor Neil Schwartz
            Rhonda Hoffman
Cover calligraphy by: Joanne Young Stephan
Text calligraphy by: Marilyn Priem
                      Joanne Young Stephan
Illustrations by: Nina Yellin
Music arranged by: Melody Yellin

* The Kugel Book - Featuring Madame á la Kugel by Nina Yellin, 1989 was the first edition from which the current book evolved.

Printed in the U.S.A.

SMYLAN REED BOOKS
Post Office Box 14311
Scottsdale, Arizona 85267-4311

DEDICATION

In memory of my parents
Betty and Frank Field and my Aunt Myrna Cohen

ACKNOWLEDGEMENTS

Thanks to all of the people who contributed information about the business of books and kugel tidbits and thanks to everyone below who contributed recipes.

Melody Yellin, Lisa Yellin, Betty Field, Myrna Cohen, Paula Costanzo, Diane Winstin, Jerry Yellin, Merle Pollack, Diane Dubin, Mel Silverman, Laurie Zellnik, Bobbi Barr, Chris Thomas, Cecile Alexander, Vivian Friedman, Sheila Goodman, Nancy Deutsch, David Deutsch, Mae Rosenthal, Barbara Telanoff, Marilyn Moskowitz, Betty Schwartz, Claire Yellin, Cindy Yellin, Gertrude Schaffer, Eileen Rosen, Barbara Polonsky, Nadine Friedman, Elaine Gross, Merle Rotman, Lee Sitron, Pearl Alcoff, Jo Urbanelli, Morna Traffas, Barbara Haber, Sophie Marcus Treibwasser, Mort Lynn, Deen Kogan, Shari Donahue and Lynne Moyle.

BUNDLES OF THANKS

Special thanks to
general all-around good guy and hubby, Steve Yellin

TABLE OF CONTENTS

INTRODUCTION

People ask me from time to time what ever possessed me to write a book about kugels, of all things! My standard answer has been the following:

Several years ago I had a family Hanukkah party and asked three of my cousins to bring a kugel, a longtime family favorite. Nadine Friedman, Eileen Rosen and Barbara Polonsky each brought a different, fabulous kugel and it made me wonder how many recipes there are in the world for this marvelous casserole. My search began and I asked everyone I knew for their recipes.

While waiting for their responses to my query, I created my own recipes. Several months later my collection included over 180 kugel recipes. Amazingly only about 20 were exact duplicates. I tested most of the recipes and fed them to friends and relatives for more than a year. They always knew, when they came to my home, what to expect for dessert, main course, side dish or a snack.

Many years ago I discovered that cookbooks are not necessarily just recipe books. All kinds of wonderful cultural, as well as culinary information, go into cookbooks, including history and family stories. The information collected about kugels was amazing and definitely something I wanted to tell the world via a cookbook.

This book answers the original five questions:

1. _**What**_ *is a kugel?*
   2. _**Where**_ *does it come from?*
      3. _**How**_ *do you say it?*
         4. _**When**_ *do you eat it and 5.* _**why**_*?*

ANSWERS

1. "What's a Kugel" and the "More Extensive Definition" will give you the most complete explanation you will probably ever see or hear.

2. Since the Middle Ages kugel history has been closely linked to the history of the Jews, their economics, and geographic locations. The history section tells all!

3. The reasons for the pronunciations "kugel, kigel and koogle" go far beyond the simple explanation whether one is an Ashkenazic Litvak or a Galitzian as you will read in "The Great Kugel Pronunciation Debate." Who these people are and who the Sephardim are is defined as well as their kugel preparation differences.

4. and 5. The answers are in the book.

The Kugel Story - Not Just Noodle Pudding is a humorous and informative Jewish cookbook with more than 175 kugel recipes plus kugel related foods. It is the second book devoted to kugel, its history and kugel trivia. The first was entitled *The Kugel Book - Featuring Madame a la Kugel.* This is the revised version, second edition.

Some very old recipes appear just as they were originally written, including one from a rare book printed in 1788. There is also a section about historic *"Kugel and Cholent."* Many of the recipes are dietetic and low in cholesterol. Although kugels are usually very nourishing, with many recipes using all four basic food groups, some of the recipes are quite rich. *"Cholesterol Watchers' Tips"* and *"Sugar Substitutions"* were added for dieters and the health conscious so they can adapt almost every recipe to their special needs.

I hope you will enjoy serving and eating kugels prepared from the recipes in this book at holiday time, at ceremonials and at any time. May all of your kugel occasions be happy ones.

KOSHER CLASSIFICATIONS

Kugels that are suitable for the following
types of meals are designated:

(M) *Milchig* or dairy (F) *Fleishig or meat*
(P) *Pareve* or neutral (foods that can be
served with any meal)

Recipes designated (T) are "*treife*" or unfit -- they are
not kosher. This is primarily a kosher cookbook,
however, for historic or humorous interest, a few *treife*
recipes appear.

OTHER NOTES

Author's favorite recipes ✡
are designated with stars.

All standard measurements in this book are American.
All temperatures are Fahrenheit.

Glossary in back of book explains terms in this book you
may not recognize.

·1·

The
Story

WHAT'S A KUGEL?

SIMPLEST DEFINITION

NOODLE PUDDING

(but it's Not Just Noodle Pudding!)

ACCORDING TO THE BRITANNICA DICTIONARY:

Definition of the word "pudding"

1. A sweetened and flavored dessert of soft food, usually farinaceous. 2. The filling inside a sausage or hot dog.* This definition would also pertain to the bread-like filling inside stuffed kishka or derma. That filling is a bread kugel type mixture!

Note: *Since this is a Jewish cookbook, I am, of course, only referring to the kosher, all-beef variety.

Definition of the word "farinaceous"

1. Consisting or made of farina. 2. Containing or yielding starch. 3. Mealy.

Definition of the word "farina"

1. A meal or flour obtained chiefly from cereals, nuts, potatoes, or Indian corn and used as a breakfast food. 2. Starch.

Please see "More Extensive Definition Of This Culinary Delight" for more details.

MORE EXTENSIVE DEFINITION
OF THIS CULINARY DELIGHT

Kugel is a light to heavy semi-moist solid bread-like
pudding or casserole-type food that is very popular in
Jewish cuisine and is usually kosher. It is extremely
versatile and can be served hot or cold as a main or
side dish, for dessert, breakfast, lunch, dinner, or at
snack time. This great crowd pleaser is often served at
Jewish holiday and ceremonial meals.

The three ingredients kugels have in common are eggs
(egg substitute or egg whites are OK to substitute in
most recipes), a starchy base and either margarine or
oil (preferably cholesterol free) or butter. Although
bread or cake-like in consistency, kugels are neither
bread nor cake. They are in a class of their own.
However, some kugels use bread or bread crumbs as a
base. More like English puddings, they sometimes have
a pie-like crust. Grains and potatoes are sometimes
used as a base giving kugel a farinaceous or farina-like
consistency.

The most frequently used starch is noodles. Kugel is
often described as *"noodle pudding."*

Yiddish definition -- (kugel) -- pudding

However, kugel originally derived its name due to its
shape, which was usually round in early kugel history.
Today kugels are prepared in many shapes.

German definition -- (koogle) -- ball, sphere,
                                globe, bullet

Hebrew definition -- (kigle) -- round

There is a theory that kugel is a traditional holiday
food because its shape is like a mound of manna. Manna
falls from the tamarisk tree in June and July and
provided nourishment for the early Hebrews during their
journey across the desert when food was scarce. They
called it "manna from heaven."

In addition to the ingredients mentioned above, fruits

16

or vegetables, dairy products, spices, nuts, and other ingredients are included in hundreds of different combinations to comprise wonderful sweet or not sweet kugels. Although some recipes are gourmet, most are very easy to prepare with as few as four ingredients. Many include all four basic food groups. The "Kugel Shopping List" details a huge variety of ingredients that are used to prepare these delicious and nutritious crowd pleasers.

Cheese-noodle kugels can be sweet or not sweet. The cheeses used are usually not stringy when melted, such as mozzarella, and are seldom sharp. When legumes (i.e. peas and beans) or tomatoes are used, the casserole would not be a kugel. If candies (such as chocolate) are included, it would be a cake (or something) but not a kugel!

Sweet kugels can be served for morning breakfast, late night breakfast, or to break the fast at sundown Yom Kippur -- the Day of Atonement. (See the *"Traditional Dairy Meal For a Crowd"* menu.) They can also be eaten at brunch, lunch, snack-time, dinner, or even as dessert. But be careful -- it is habit-forming and absolutely irresistible. Beware of leftovers!

Kugels that are not sweet would be best served as a main course at lunch-time or as a side dish at dinner with meat, poultry, or fish and fruit and salad.

Kugels are either baked in an oven, steamed in the center of a cholent (stew) or cooked stove-top in a heavy iron skillet. Usually they are baked in a square or rectangular-shaped pan -- sizes varying from 8" x 8" to 11" x 16" -- unless you are a caterer, then they are HUGE! (See the **Cool Whip Jygunda Kugel** recipe). Occasionally they will be baked in muffin tins or round pans. I feel that 2 inches high is best, but my friend, Mel Silverman likes kugels that are much higher. Servings are usually cut into 2-3 inch squares.

Kugels are served throughout the year and are especially popular at holiday meals. During the eight days of Passover, kugels made from matzah and its derivatives are served (see the Passover Kugel section in this book).

To break the 24-hour fast during Yom Kippur a dairy meal including cheese kugel is enjoyed by many. This delightful meal is also frequently served at the celebration after the confirmation of graduating Hebrew school students during the holiday of Shavuot -- the Festival of the Giving of the Law -- the Ten Commandments and the Torah. As Shavuot is the Festival of the Fruits, a cheese kugel topped with fruit would be ideal to serve.

Before the holiday of Sukkot -- the Festival of the Fall Harvest -- sukkahs made of vines and dried leaves are set up. They are a reminder of the small huts that the ancient Jews in the wilderness and the harvesters lived in. A large variety of fruits and vegetables are used to decorate the sukkah where small meals are eaten. A suggested addition to the Sukkot menu is the Dried Fruit and Nut Mix Kugel. Fruity parve kugel is also often served with traditional dinners including meat or poultry for Rosh Hashanah (Jewish New Year). Hanukkah would be a good time to serve potato kugel. You can use the same batter to make potato latkes (see Hanukkah, Latkes, and Kugel chapter).

There are no set rules as to how or when kugel should be served or eaten. Usually it is eaten with a fork, but if cold and solid, it can be eaten with your fingers, like a sandwich -- as long as no one is looking!

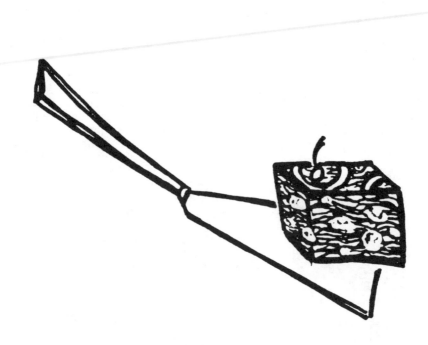

The First Time I Saw Kugel

HINTS

1. <u>Read entire recipe</u> before starting to prepare and prepare as written.

2. <u>EGGS</u> -- Also see in index "About Eggs," "Cholesterol Watchers' Tips" and Substitutions," "No egg kugels."

   <u>Separating eggs</u>. You can remove egg yolk that has gotten into the white while separating eggs by dipping a piece of the shell into the bowl. Yolk will just slide right onto it. Of course, if your problem is that a piece of **shell** has fallen into your egg white, lots of luck getting it out -- it's not as easy.

   <u>Buying and storing eggs</u>. Never buy eggs that have not been refrigerated and be sure to put them into your refrigerator as soon as possible. They should be stored in their own carton with the pointed end down so that they will not lose vitamins. They will keep for 4-5 weeks. Raw egg whites keep a week to 10 days if refrigerated in a tightly covered container.

   <u>Egg whites</u> can be frozen in ice cube trays and defrosted as needed. Refrigerate unbroken raw yolks covered with water in a tightly covered container. Drain and use within 2-3 days.

   Always use a glass, not plastic, metal or wood bowl when whipping egg whites.

   <u>Freshness</u> of an egg can be determined by immersing it in a pan of cool, salted water. If it sinks, it is fresh; if it rises to the surface, throw it away.

Note: The average hen lays 277 eggs a year or enough so you can make one kugel each week for a year!

3. **Cooking noodles**. Add 1 tablespoon of oil to the water to prevent noodles from sticking. Run water through the noodles, after draining, to keep them from sticking together.

    Overcooking noodles slightly for some recipes will make the kugel lighter. Undercook noodles slightly in recipes with a lot of liquid or canned fruit.

4. **Remove the lid of a steaming pot** by tilting it away from your face.

5. **Toppings**: Most sweet kugels are delicious when topped with sour cream or fruit toppings. Whipped cream on some would make a wonderful dessert. See "Make a Plain Kugel Fancy" for designs.

6. **Cottage cheese will last longer** in refrigerator if you "burp" the air out as you would with a plastic storage container. Turn the container upside down and return to the refrigerator. This will prevent air from touching the cheese and it will keep far longer than if stored upright.

7. **Butter will soften quickly** if you grate it while hard and cold. Or microwave at 30% power for 1 minute.

8. **Cream cheese will soften quickly** microwaved at 30% power for 2 to 2-1/2 minutes for 8 ounces. A 3-ounce package will soften in 1-1/2 to 2 minutes.

9. **Onion chopping hints** -- prevent tears by: Cutting root end off first...Peeling under cold running water...Using a food processor... Periodically rinsing hands under cold water... Refrigerating or freezing for 4 or 5 minutes before chopping...Wearing contact lenses.

10. **When chopping and grating**, use the food processor. It's fabulous! But for dicing, use a knife.

11. **Cooking methods** -- kugels are usually baked but they are sometimes steamed or cooked on the stovetop in a well-oiled heavy iron frying pan.

STOVE-TOP COOKING

Many noodle, bread and potato kugel recipes can be prepared stove-top

Pour mixture into a well-oiled deep skillet, press mixture down and cover pan. Cook over slow fire, do not stir. When mixture starts to set, shake pan. When firm and crusty, put a plate or fry pan lid on top. Hold lid with one hand and flip pan upside down. Let kugel come out of pan. Then carefully slide kugel back into pan, top side down, and brown so the entire kugel is crusty. Put a plate on top of flipped kugel, if necessary, to hold it down while browning the final portion.

12. **Save a pot**. Melt butter or margarine in the same pan you will be baking in.

13. **Saute vegetables** -- use 2 tablespoons oil to start with, then use 2 or 3 tablespoons of water if too dry and steam saute to complete. You will save calories. Do not overcook vegetables!

14. **To absorb cabbage cooking odor**, place a small tin cup or can half filled with vinegar on stove or counter near where cabbage will be cooking.

15. **Brown sugar** -- Brown sugar won't harden if an apple slice or prunes are placed in the container. But if it does harden -- place a slice of soft bread in the package of hardened brown sugar and sugar will soften in a couple of hours. Or use a grater and grate the needed amount of hardened brown sugar.

16. **Grater cleaning** -- use a toothbrush to clean lemon rind, cheese, onion, etc. out of grater before washing it.

17. **Individual servings** -- bake kugel in muffin tins for 1/4 less time than what is called for in recipe or until mixture is set.

18. **Freezing instructions**:

    Leftovers -- wrap tightly in freezer wrap, freezer proof plastic container or plastic wrap and foil and freeze for up to four weeks.

    Unbaked kugel -- cover mixture with freezer wrap, or with plastic wrap and then aluminum foil.

Freeze in pan for up to four weeks. Thaw overnight and bake according to instructions in recipe.

Baked whole kugel -- bake 15 minutes less than recipe calls for. Cool. Wrap in freezer wrap or plastic and then aluminum foil. Freeze for up to four weeks. Place thawed kugel in preheated oven and bake 15 minutes at temperature recommended in recipe.

Keep kugels up to four weeks in the freezer. Beyond four weeks they may acquire a refrigerator taste.

Do not freeze potato kugels because they will be watery when defrosted.

Vegetable kugels, when indicated in recipe, should not be frozen. They will be too watery after defrosting.

MAKE A PLAIN KUGEL FANCY

Top a kugel with fresh, canned or prepared fruit, cinnamon, sugar (confectioners, brown or white refined) jam or cereal, sour cream or yogurt. (See Toppings in index).

For fancier dessert kugels, use the diagrams below. Use drained crushed or chunk pineapple, or prepared cherry, apple or blueberry pie topping. Substitute apple pie filling for crushed pineapple, if desired in diagrams below. Sprinkle slivered almonds over any of the toppings for an added touch.

EASY

Cover with cherries and scatter pineapple chunks on top or make design with cherries and pineapple as shown here.

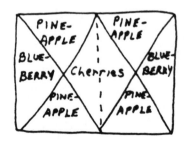

RED, WHITE AND BLUE

Cover entire kugel with sour cream. Place blueberries where stars would be and sprinkle slivered almonds. Every other stripe will be cherries.

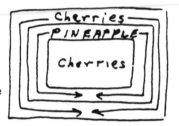

HARLEQUIN

Draw a line down the center. Draw two large "X's." Fill with crushed pineapple, cherries, and blueberries.

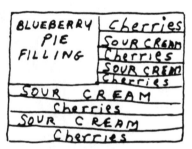

CHOLESTEROL WATCHERS' TIPS

When some people hear the word "kugel" they shriek and imagine red lights flashing "stop" and flags waving a warning "high fat and cholesterol food." I say, "No, no, no — it is not necessary to feel that way. Kugels can be very nourishing and part of a very healthy diet."

The Food and Drug Administration says people should "eat more fruits, vegetables, cereal grains and starches (all of which are in kugels), which have less fat (particularly saturated fat) and no cholesterol, and by choosing vegetable oils such as:

1. Safflower, sunflower, corn, and soybean oils, which have higher levels of polyunsaturated fatty acids and low levels of saturated fatty acids. In addition, peanut, olive, canola are good oils.

   Canola oil is considered to be the best and corn oil second best. Both canola and corn oil are rich sources of vitamin E. Canola is lowest in saturated (bad) fat (6%) and highest in beneficial mono unsaturated fat and is thought to help decrease cholesterol.

   Pure vegetable oil may contain tropical oils of coconut, palm, and palm oil if contents are not specified and may be high in saturated fats.

2. **Margarine** -- Soft tub margarines are higher in (good) polyunsaturates than hardened ones. Use a light, corn or canola oil margarine.

3. **Butter** -- Light butter contains half the fat of butter or margarine and is low in sodium and cholesterol.

4. **Eggs, whole** -- According to the U.S.D.A., "Eggs are an important part of a healthy diet. They are nutrient-dense, providing essential vitamins and minerals, economical, low-calorie, and a source of high-quality protein."

   Eggs are 22% lower in cholesterol than previously thought according to the U.S.D.A. -- and 96% fat-free of saturated fat. Eggs contain mono-unsaturated fats, which current research suggests is healthful.

THE AVERAGE SERVING OF KUGEL
CONTAINS ONLY 1/4 OF AN EGG.

However, if your doctor strongly advises not to eat eggs or if you want to cut back on calories or adhere to your weekly egg allotment (3-4 large or 4-5 medium whole eggs per week are recommended for the average diet), use two egg whites for every egg in a recipe. Or discard every other yolk and substitute a teaspoon of polyunsaturated oil for each discarded yolk in recipes. Commercial egg substitutes are also OK to use.

A LARGE EGG CONTAINS 80 CALORIES,
60 ARE IN THE YOLK

Also see listed in index: "No Egg Kugels", "About Eggs", "Hints and Substitutions"

5.   **Creams and cheeses**

For lower cholesterol, substitute the foods listed below. However, recipes may taste slightly blander than if recipe is prepared as originally stated.

Sour cream -- light sour cream or yogurt
Cottage cheese -- low-fat cottage cheese
Cream cheese -- light cream cheese, farmer
        cheese, imitation cream cheese, low fat
        cottage cheese, part skim ricotta, nonfat
        yogurt cheese*

* To Make Yogurt cheese -- Use coffee filter in strainer positioned over bowl. Pour nonfat yogurt into filter and let drain overnight (refrigerated).

6.   **Additional Tips:**

Use a non-stick baking spray such as Pam to grease your pans.

Steam vegetables instead of sauteing to save calories.

Milk -- use skim or low-fat (2 percent).

Substitute orange juice for oil
i.e.: 1/4 cup orange juice = 1/4 cup oil

SUGAR AND CINNAMON

For hundreds of years cinnamon and sugar have been used more often than any other spices in kugels.

Cinnamon has been used extensively in Jewish cuisine since before King Solomon's time. Jews have always favored the flavor or sugar, which they brought to the western world in the 14th Century. Trade with spice- producing countries in the Far East had been an important occupation of the Jews for centuries.

SUGAR SUBSTITUTES

1. Use heat-stable sugar substitutes*, such as Sunette Sweet One. Use the equivalent of what your recipe calls for in sugar.

   * Sugar substitutes that contain Nutrasweet are not heat-stable and they lose their sweetness when baked for a long period of time.

2. Use half sugar and make up difference in taste using sugar substitute to cut calories and keep the sugar taste.

3. Fructose (natural sugar found in fresh fruits and honey), or Sucanat (evaporated sugar cane) have half the calories of sugar, but the taste is not the same.

4. Use "sugar free" and "in their own juices" canned fruits and jellies.

5. Use one can of frozen, undiluted concentrated fruit juice for one cup of sugar.

BEING KOSHER

Kugels are usually kosher. Dietary Laws of Kashruth are taken from the Bible in the Five Books of Moses and have been followed for thousands of years. The laws apply to all daily requirements of Jewish ritual life. Kosher or *Kasher* in Hebrew means "fit" or "proper." Any health value is considered coincidental.

To prepare a strictly "kosher" recipe you should check labels on packaged grocery products to be sure they are marked with a "K" or a "U" in a circle. If you will be preparing a *pareve* recipe, also look for a "P" on the packaging. During Passover, holiday products should be marked "Kosher for Passover."

In the kitchen, two separate sets of dishes, pots and pans, silverware and utensils are kept for dairy and meat meals. To make the kitchen kosher for the holiday of Passover in an Ashkenazik Jewish home, dishes used at other times during the year are stored away and two other sets of dishes are used. Before Passover the kitchen is thoroughly cleaned so no bread crumbs remain.

During Passover, matzah and its derivatives are used since leavened bread is not permitted during the holiday. Traditionally only root vegetables are served at Ashkenazic Passover meals. Other foods used must be approved "Kosher for Passover."

Foods permitted and not permitted, according to the Laws of Kashruth, are listed below.

FOODS THAT ARE PERMITTED

1. *Foods that can be eaten in their natural state*, such as fruits, vegetables, nuts, grains, eggs, fish, etc. These foods are *pareve* (pronounced par-reh-vuh or par-vuh) meaning neutral in English. They can therefore be eaten with dairy or meat meals.

2. *Dairy Products* -- These and meals prepared with these products are called *milchig* (pronounced mil-hig), meaning milk. The word denotes dairy foods, dishes and utensils.

3. *Meat and poultry* -- Meats must be from only peaceful, cloven-hoofed animals who graze and chew their cud -- cows, sheep, goats, and deer. Some parts are not kosher.

    Poultry must be barnyard birds, such as chickens, ducks, turkeys, geese.

    Birds and animals must be killed quickly and painlessly under religious supervision. They must be thoroughly bled (since the consumption of blood is strictly forbidden). They must also be salted, cleaned and inspected. Liver and certain other cuts of meat must be broiled. These foods are *fleishig* (flay-shig) meaning flesh. The word denotes meat food, dishes, and utensils.

Note: Dairy substitutes can be used in a pareve meal as long as they are certified kosher and pareve. The federal government allows sodium caseinate (milchig) in what are called "non-dairy" powders. "Coffee Mate" is not milchig or dairy for this reason.

FOODS THAT ARE NOT PERMITTED:

1. Pork products, meat from carnivorous animals and birds, shellfish, fish without scales and fins. Almost all crawling and swarming things such as insects, snakes, and reptiles. These are "treife" (unfit).

2. Dairy products and meat cannot be <u>cooked</u> together. Dairy and meat cannot be <u>eaten</u> together in the same meal. Exodus 23:19: "You shall not cook a kid in its mother's milk."

EGGS AND KASHRUTH

Although eggs are sold in the dairy section of the grocery store, eggs are not considered, in Jewish law, to be "dairy." They are neutral or *pareve* and can be served and/or cooked with either meat *(fleishig)* or dairy *(milchig)* meals.

Since the consumption of blood is strictly forbidden, an egg with a blood spot would be unkosher and should be discarded along with any food that it touches. Today hens and roosters are separated on modern chicken farms so there is no reason to believe that a blood spotted egg would have been fertilized. However, an egg like this would probably come from a diseased chicken.

To protect consumers, egg farms candle (or hold a light up to) their eggs so that they can tell if there are any spots in them. However, some do a better job than others and occasionally a bad egg is found. In order to be safe, a kosher cook should first crack each egg to be used into a cup. It should be checked and, if satisfactory, it can be used.

Her
  egg
    shaped
      face is
        crowned
          with
          golden
            ringlets
            of noodles.
              She has lem-
                on shaped
                eyes, dark
                as luscious
                blueberries.
                When she laughs
                almond tears fall
                past her plump,
                rosy cheeks to
                her cherry red
                lips. Her comp-
                lexion is smooth
                as milk and honey.
                Madame à la Kugel
                has a cute little
                nose with raisin
                shaped nostrils to
                savor the exquisite
                aroma of kugel baking.
                Ears resembling apple
                halves hear rave reviews
                from fans. With a person-
                ality as sweet as sugar, she
                is a peach of a gal and her
                friends are just nuts about her.

Madame à la Kugel

KUGEL SHOPPING LIST

The following list is intended only to point out the extensive variety of ingredients used to make kugels. But fear not! You do not have to have all of these ingredients at your fingertips to consider yourself a kugel maven (expert)!

BASIC INGREDIENTS FOR MOST POPULAR KUGELS

Vanilla, cinnamon
Eggs or egg whites
Butter or margarine
Sugar -- white, granulated
Apples, crushed pineapple
Noodles -- fine, medium, wide
Raisins -- black or white seedless
Cream cheese, cottage cheese, sour cream

OTHER INGREDIENTS USED

Noodles   Spaghetti, whole wheat, spinach, Passover, no yolk, orzo

Flours   Presifted, unbleached or whole wheat

Breads   Crumbs, loaf breads, rolls, matzah

Cereals   Corn Flakes, Frosted Flakes, farina, graham cracker crumbs

Grains	Bulgur, millet, pearl barley, rice (brown or white, not instant), grits, kasha (groats)
Potatoes	White, sweet

Dairy Products

Cheeses:
    cheddar, parmesan, ricotta, farmer, pot or dry cottage, muenster

Creams:
    light, heavy, half and half, pareve non-dairy creamer, whipped topping
Milk:
    powdered dry, liquid whole or skim
Yogurt:
    banana, plain, vanilla, raspberry

Oils	Canola, safflower, corn, olive, peanut, sunflower
Sweeteners	Sugar -- brown, white, confectioners, honey, heat-stable artificial sweetener, juices
Spices	Salt, pepper, paprika ginger, allspice, nutmeg, cinnamon, cloves, coriander, cumin
Herbs	Dill, parsley -- dry or fresh
Extracts	Vanilla, almond, vanilla-butternut, brandy
Baking agents	Baking powder
Soups	Broth -- chicken Dry soup mix -- chicken, onion
Puddings	Vanilla, banana

Fruits

Fruit Sauces:
    Applesauce
Fruit Juices or Peels:
    Apple, apricot nectar, lemon, orange
Fruit Jellies and Jams:
    Apricot, pineapple, prickly pear

More Fruit	Fresh (F), Dried (D), Canned (C), Prepared Pie Filling (PF):

Apples (F), (PF) -- sweet or sour
Apricots (D), (F)
Grapes (F), (C) red, green,
Coconut (D)
Pineapple (F) -- sliced (C), chunk (C) crushed (C)
Oranges (C), (F) -- mandarin
Peaches (F), (C)
Cherries (C) maraschino, Queen Ann, black
Dates (D)
Prunes (D)
Fruit Cocktail (C)
Plums (F)

Nuts and Seeds	Almonds, walnuts, pecans, mixed sunflower seeds
Vegetables	Carrots, broccoli, cabbage, spinach, zucchini, onions, mushrooms, celery, red and green bell pepper, cauliflower and asparagus?
Wines	White, sweet red
Grebenes	Cracklings
Fish and Meats	Cooked, smoked or canned fish, liver, chicken

KUGEL
PRONUNCIATION
DEBATE

THE GREAT KUGEL PRONUNCIATION DEBATE

Kugel, Koogle or Kigle?

Most people, including me, say *kugel*, -- the "U" is pronounced the same as the "oo" in the word *good*. This is the Litvak (Lithuanian) and Yiddish form of pronunciation. A Galitzian or Galitzianer (a person from Galacia -- an area stretching across southeastern Poland to southwestern Russia, whose borders have changed frequently throughout history) would say *kigle* (sounds like wiggle) which is the Hebrew pronunciation. The German pronunciation is *koogle*. The "oo" is pronounced the same as the "oo" in the word "coo," the sound doves and babies make. Cows do it too but they put an *mmmm* in front. "Mmmm" is, of course, the sound people make when they eat kugel.

What it really boils down to is accent differences according to where one is from, or one's ancestors. According to my friend, Natalie Knecht, everyone where she grew up (Upper Darby, PA) said kigle. In Chicago, Sheila Goodman said everyone also called it kigle. In fact, when she was growing up, she thought *kugel* was a sweet *kigle,* but she had never tasted a sweet *kugel* until she moved to the east.

Lithuania and Galacia are areas that were very heavily populated by Jews. The Litvak Jews were very influential in their communities and were very much involved in business. They were highly regarded and quite sophisticated and it was their Yiddish pronunciation "kugel" that was considered to be "proper."

36

The Galitzians were primarily Hassidim or Hassidic. The Hassidim (also spelled C-h-a-s-s-i-d-i-m) are a sect of very pious Orthodox Jews that was formed in 1750. The men, who wear long beards and earlocks, are quite distinctive in their striking black coats and hats. In Galacia, they were a folksy, peasant-type people. A Galitzian might argue that the Hebrew pronunciation "kigle" is the only way to say the word.

Now you might ask the question, "What happens to the pronunciation when one's mother is a Galitzian and one's father is a Litvak?" This happened to my cousin, Paula Costanzo. I think it has something to do with which parent has the dominant pronunciation genes!

KUGEL FOR A CROWD

Kugel is absolutely the ultimate Jewish crowd pleaser. It was always served by my mother whenever there was a family gathering while I was growing up. And today it is still a family favorite, especially "Mom Field's Cherry Kugel."

Ceremonial gatherings where kugel is served are usually a huge success. Babies are practically weaned on it. After all, it is first introduced into their lives when they are just a few days old, at a boy baby's "Ben Zochor." This is a party held on the first Friday after his birth. Eight days after the little guy is born, there will be a B'rith Millah or Bris, the Rite of Circumcision. The relatives will show up again and kugel will again be a part of the goodies. The baby probably isn't in the mood to party at this point and wishes the relatives would all just go away. After a bit of a cry, he quietly drinks his bottle and goes to sleep.

One month later, there's another party and this time he is *in the mood!* This is the Pidyon-Ha-Ben, the Redemption of the Firstborn Son -- a ceremony dating back to the sojourn in Egypt. He takes his first good whiff of kugel and he is a *very* happy child. He can't wait to sink his gums into it.

In families who are not Orthodox, a party is also given for a newborn girl child after the Simhat Bat (naming ceremony). If she becomes a Bat Mitzvah, usually at age thirteen, kugel might be served at the celebration after the ceremony which marks her as an adult member of the community. The same for a thirteen year old boy at his Bar Mitzvah celebration. Kugel will again, perhaps, be served at their wedding.

Kugel will probably be eaten from time to time throughout their entire lives. When they die, the relatives will, no doubt, be eating it again at the gathering after their funerals.

PLANNING A LARGE PARTY?

Serve Cool Whip Jygunda Kugel on p. 39 or consider using all of the recipes in this book and serve with the following:

ELEPHANT STEW (T)

1 elephant (medium size)
2 rabbits (optional)
pepper
salt

Cut elephant into bite-sized pieces. This should take about two months. Add enough brown gravy to cover. Cook over high flame for about four weeks or until tender.

This recipe will serve about 3,800, but if more are expected, two rabbits may be added. Do this only if absolutely necessary as most people to not like hare in their stew.

COOL WHIP JYGUNDA KUGEL (M) ✡

Tastes like a cheesecake

1 lb. thin noodles, cooked and drained
     (yes, just 1 pound!)
3 cups sugar
16-18 extra large eggs *
1-1/2 tablespoons vanilla extract
3 lb. whipped cream cheese *
3 lb. sour cream *
1 lb. butter, softened *
1 lg. container Cool Whip *
     cinnamon

Preheat oven to 350 degrees.   45 to 60 servings

Cream together sugar, eggs and vanilla. Beat in cream
cheese and butter and sour cream. Add noodles and toss.
Fold in cool whip. Pour into aluminum throw away turkey
baking pan sprayed with non-stick baking spray (to save
calories). Sprinkle with cinnamon. Bake one hour and
20 minutes to 1-1/2 hours until set. Or pour into THREE
9" x 13" baking pans (sprayed with non-stick baking
spray). Sprinkle with cinnamon. Bake one hour.

* To reduce fats and cholesterol I use:

          8 whole eggs plus 16 egg whites
          large container light cool whip
          1-1/2 lbs. regular cream cheese
          1-1/2 lbs. light cream cheese
          1-1/2 lbs. regular sour cream
          1-1/2 lbs. light sour cream
          1 lb. light soft margarine

TRADITIONAL DAIRY MEAL
MENU FOR A CROWD

If you start early, this meal could last all day!
Serve with dairy noodle kugel (fruity or not).

Fish:

Smoked	Kippered salmon, nova and/or belly lox, sable, chubs, white fish
Herring	Pickled, plain, in cream sauce, schmaltz, and/or chopped
Fish Salad	Tuna, salmon, white fish, kosher mock seafood

Dairy Products:

Cheeses	Cream cheese, cottage cheese, muenster, American, Swiss
Creams	Sour cream, half and half
Butter	Sweet or lightly salted

Fruits: Assorted whole fresh fruit or fruit salad (don't forget the kiwi!)

Vegetables: Cold sliced cucumbers, onions (Bermuda or purple), tomatoes

Breads: Bagels (assorted), rye bread (plain and seeded) pumpernickel or black bread

Desserts: Jello molds*, miniature danish, strudel, apple cake, ruggalah, schnecken and mandel broit, mints, and nuts.

Beverages: Juice, milk, soda, coffee, tea, water, seltzer

*Use kosher gelatin for molds

40

BAGELS (P)

"Lox without bagels", you say? IMPOSSIBLE! Bagels are absolutely a must with the Traditional Dairy Meal menu.

Everyone seems to have his or her own favorite way to eat bagels and lox. I like to eat it open faced on a toasted bagel that has been spread with some cream cheese, not too thick, about one ounce of lox on each half, and topped with slices of cucumber, tomato and onion. Sometimes I will add a slice of cheese or a little bit of another smoked fish.

The word "bagel" is Yiddish for roll. The art of bagel baking was brought to New York from eastern Europe by the Jewish immigrants probably around 1900. The flavored varieties like pumpernickel, garlic, rye and egg are definitely American. Until the last 10 years or so, bagels were almost totally unknown by people who did not live near the big cities and by those who were not Jewish. Today bagels can be found in almost every city in this country, thanks to a famous fast-food chain. They are also usually available in grocery stores in the frozen food section, if not in their bakery department. Some bakeries specialize in bagel baking where this chewy bread that is crusty on the outside and soft on the inside and shaped like a donut can be purchased fresh and hot straight from the oven.

4	cups bread flour
3/4	cup warm water
1	envelope fresh active dry yeast
2	teaspoons sugar
1/4	cup oil
2	large eggs
1-3/4	teaspoons salt

Pour the yeast into 1/4 cup of warm water with 1 teaspoon of sugar. Let this sit for about 10 minutes until it becomes foamy. Add the rest of the sugar and water, oil, eggs and salt. Sift flour into a large bowl and make a well in the center. Mix together with a spoon and then with your hands until a dough is formed. Knead the dough on a lightly floured board for about 10 minutes until it is smooth and not sticky. Add a little more dough to board as necessary. Place dough into a clean oiled bowl, cover with a damp cloth and allow to rise in a warm area (like near a dryer that is running or on top of a refrigerator) for about an hour or until doubled in size.

Knead the dough again for a minute or so and then form a thick log. Cut into 12 pieces with a knife that has been coated with flour. Roll out each piece into a 5 inch length that is about 3/4 inch in diameter, form a circle and pinch the ends together. Place on a floured board, cover and allow to rise for about 15 more minutes.

THE NEXT STEPS FOR BAGEL MAKING

2   quarts water
1-1/2 tablespoons sugar
1   large egg, beaten with a pinch of salt

Preheat oven to 400 degrees.

Bring water and sugar to a boil. Turn heat down to medium and gently drop in 3 or 4 bagels. Simmer for a minute and then turn each bagel onto other side with a slotted spoon. Simmer for another minute. Remove bagels with slotted spoon and place on paper towels. Repeat with the rest of the bagels. Place on a greased baking sheet. Brush with egg, sprinkle with poppy or sesame seeds if desired and bake 25 minutes or until browned. Bagels can be frozen. They are great when warmed or sliced and toasted before serving.

CHOPPED HERRING (P)

1 small jar of herring filets, in wine sauce
  onions from jar of herring
2 hard boiled eggs
1 tart apple, pared
3 tablespoons dry bread crumbs

Drain the herring and chop with eggs and onions to a coarse consistency. Add grated apples and bread crumbs. Stir thoroughly and chill. Serve with bagel chips, crackers or party breads.

JEWISH APPLE CAKE (P)

cinnamon-sugar mixture made with:
      5 teaspoons sugar
      2 teaspoons cinnamon
4-5   apples, peeled, cored and thinly sliced
3   cups sifted flour
2   cups sugar
1   cup oil
4   eggs
1/4   cup orange juice
3   teaspoons baking powder
2-1/2 teaspoons vanilla
pinch of salt

Preheat oven to 350 degrees.   12 servings

Mix apples with cinnamon-sugar mixture. Sift flour and baking powder together. Add remaining ingredients and beat together. Pour 1/3 of the batter into greased tube pan; add 1/2 of the apples. Repeat layers, finishing with batter. Bake 1-1/2 hours.

RUGGELAH (M)

Ruggelah is probably the best known Jewish cookie. However, it is frequently confused with schnecken. The dough is different for each. Ruggelah is baked in either a crescent or log shape and is prepared with a wide variety of fillings.

DOUGH:

8 ounces cream cheese, softened
2 sticks margarine, softened
2 cups unbleached flour

In mixing bowl or food processor, cream the margarine and cream cheese. Beat in the flour, a little at a time. Knead the dough lightly until all the flour is mixed in. Divide dough into four balls. Refrigerate two hours or up to two days. Roll each portion into a 9 inch circle on a board dusted lightly with flour or powdered sugar until about 1/8 inch thick. If the dough is sticky, dust it with flour. Cut circle into triangles with a pastry wheel or knife into 12 pie-shaped wedges.

RAISIN AND NUT FILLING

1/2 cup sugar
1   tablespoon cinnamon
1   cup finely chopped walnuts
1/2 cup raisins
Preheat oven to 350 degrees.   Makes 48 pieces.

Combine sugar and cinnamon.   Sprinkle over prepared
rolled out and cut dough then sprinkle nuts and raisins.
Press ingredients down into dough with rolling pin.
Separate the dough (cut through again if necessary).

** Beginning at the wide edge, roll dough up toward the
point, folding into a crescent shape, and pinch in the
ends to seal.   Place on ungreased cookie sheets about
1 inch apart with point of triangle down.   Sprinkle with
sugar if powdered sugar was not used when rolling out
the dough.   Refrigerate 20 minutes before baking.
Repeat until all dough and filling is used. Bake 20-25
minutes or until golden, brushing with melted butter
after 15 minutes if desired.

JAM FILLING

Combine 1 cup ground almonds and 1 cup strawberry,
apricot or raspberry jam or preserves **OR** just use 2 cups
of jam or preserves without nuts.

Divide into four portions and spread on rolled out and
cut dough. ** Follow instructions above.

CHOCOLATE CHIP FILLING

Divide 2 cups miniature semisweet chocolate chips into
four portions and spread on rolled out and cut dough.
** Follow instructions above.

Note: Rolled out dough can be cut into strips, spread
with filling and rolled into log shapes.   Slice 1-1/2
inch pieces and bake.

44

Absolutely
Absolutely

SCHNECKEN (M)

DOUGH:

3   cups flour, unbleached and presifted
3   teaspoons sugar *Splenda-*
1/2 teaspoon salt
2   sticks butter or margarine
2   eggs, beaten
1   cup light cream
1   package fresh active yeast

Cut butter into flour, salt and sugar. Combine eggs and cream. Add egg mixture to dough mixture and blend well. Sprinkle dry yeast over dough and knead so that it holds together. Divide into six balls. Place in a bowl, cover with plastic wrap and refrigerate overnight. Roll out each ball into a circle on a floured board.

FILLING:

1-1/2 cups sugar
1   cup crushed pecans or walnuts (optional)
3-4   tablespoons cinnamon

Preheat oven to 350 degrees.   Makes 48 pieces.

Combine sugar with cinnamon and nuts. Divide into six portions. Spread the mixture out on a board. Place one circle of rolled out dough on top and press dough down into mixture. Turn dough to coat other side. Cut coated dough with a pastry cutter into eight pie-shaped wedges. Roll each wedge, starting at the wide edge. Turn edges in, if desired, to make a crescent shape. Place on greased cookie sheet for 20 minutes or until golden.

AUNT MYRNA'S MANDEL BROIT (P)

Absolutely

This is the Jewish version of the Italian Biscotti.

1   cup sugar plus 2 tablespoons for sprinkling
3   eggs, beaten
1   cup oil
1   teaspoon vanilla
1/2   teaspoon baking powder
2-3/4 cups flour, unbleached, presifted
1   cup slivered almonds or chocolate chips

Preheat oven to 350 degrees   Makes about 36 cookies

Beat together eggs, vanilla and oil. Using a spoon and your hands when necessary, add 1 cup sugar, flour and baking powder to egg mixture. Add nuts or chocolate chips. Knead dough to get everything mixed together thoroughly. Dough will be oily. Divide into two balls. Form long loaves about 4 inches wide and about 1-1/2 inches high; sprinkle with remaining sugar; place on cookie sheet. Bake 30 minutes. Remove from oven and slice into 1-inch bars. Lay cookies on their sides and bake 10 more minutes to brown.

LIME SOUR CREAM MOLD (M)

2   packages kosher lime gelatin
1   pint sour cream
1   cup boiling water
1   small jar maraschino cherries, drained and
      quartered
1/2 cup coarsely chopped walnuts
1   large can crushed pineapple, do not drain

Dissolve gelatin in boiling water. Cool until syrupy like egg whites. Add crushed pineapple with its juice. Beat in sour cream until smooth. Add nuts and cherries. Pour into a well oiled 2-quart mold. Chill until set. Invert onto serving dish. Serves 8-10

MANDARIN ORANGE DESSERT MOLD (M)

2 small packages kosher orange gelatin
2 cups boiling water
1 11 oz. can mandarin oranges
1 pint orange sherbert, softened

Dissolve gelatin in boiling water. Drain oranges into a measuring cup. Add enough water to equal one cup. Add to gelatin. Chill until slightly thickened. Blend in sherbert and mandarin oranges. Pour into a 1-1/2 quart mold. Chill until firm. Invert onto serving dish. Serves 8-10.

Headline seen in popular newspaper

"KUGEL MAKES IT BIG OFF BROADWAY"

The romantic comedy entitled "Beau Jest", produced by Arthur Cantor has been showing "off Broadway" in New York since October, 1991 at the Lambs Theater. Kugel has an important role in the show and it is served during intermission.

This delightful show came to the Society Hill Playhouse in Philadelphia for six months in September of 1992. The playhouse sponsored a kugel contest and produced its very own "Kugel Contest Cookbook." The following recipe is from that book.

Absolutely   Absolutely

SAVORY SOCIETY HILL KUGEL (M)

1/2	lb. wide egg noodles, cooked and drained
2	cups sliced whole scallions
4	garlic cloves, peeled and crushed
1/4	cup butter
4	eggs, beaten
1	lb. creamed cottage cheese (at room temperature)
1	cup light sour cream (at room temperature)
1/2	teaspoon salt
1/4	teaspoon pepper
1-1/2	cups Muenster cheese, grated
1/4	cup wheat germ mixed with 1/4 teaspoon paprika

Preheat oven to 350 degrees.   15 servings

Saute scallions and garlic in melted butter until they are limp. Toss the noodles with the scallion mixture. Combine eggs, cottage cheese, sour cream, salt and pepper and stir into the noodle mixture. Pour into a lightly greased 9" x 13" baking dish. Sprinkle top with Muenster cheese, then dust the cheese evenly with the wheat germ mixture. Bake 40-45 minutes.

Some Very Old Recipes

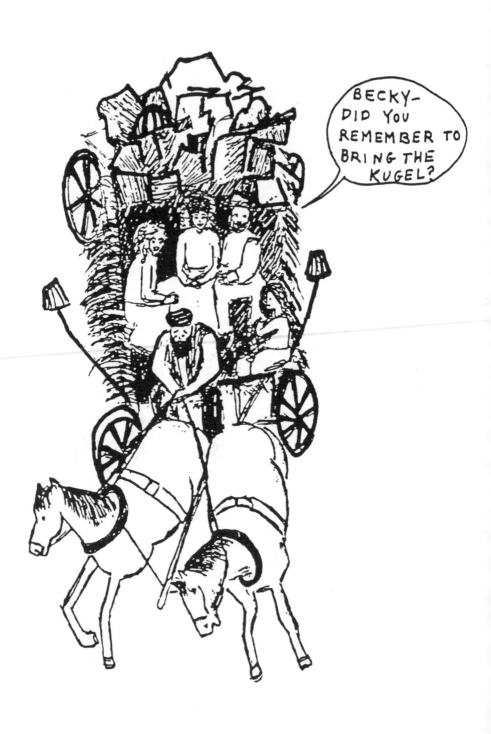

HISTORY

THE ASHKENAZIM

Kugels have been in existence at least since the Middle Ages. Vegetables were available only during the harvest season in many areas and were not considered to be very important in most Ashkenazic Jewish homes. In their place, kugels were substituted.

"Ashkenaz" is the old Hebrew word meaning "Germany." The term "Ashkenazim" refers to Jewish people originally from along the southern borders of Germany and from Jewish centers along the Rhine River, where they settled by the 10th Century. In addition to Central and Eastern Europe, the Ashkenazim are now from, or are descendants of people from the Americas, Southern Africa, and Australia.

During the next several hundred years, after the 10th Century, migrations brought the majority of the Ashkenazic settlers to Poland, Lithuania, Bohemia and Russia. The Yiddish language was developed during this period of migration. It is a combination of the ancient language Hebrew, medieval or high German, and bits of local vernacular. Kugel is a Yiddish word.

In 1,100 C.E., kugels were described in Germany as bread. The recipes traveled eastward from Germany along with the Ashkenazic settlers and eventually they made their way into Russia where most kugels are not sweet. The only sweetness would come from the occasional addition of raisins. In 1,500 C.E. Polish Jews were making matzah farfel kugels and they were possibly the first made for Passover.

American Jewish cooking today is influenced primarily by Eastern European or Ashkenazic cuisine (German, Polish, and Russian). Most of the kugels that we are familiar with today are Ashkenazic.

The first kugel recipes to be printed in America were in the _Settlement Cookbook,_ published in 1903 by Mrs. Simon Kinder. This book consists primarily of German recipes. It is not a "kosher" cookbook and recipes in it may be _treife._ The book was written to raise money for the poor, newly arrived Russian immigrants.

The following recipes are written just as they originally appeared.

NOODLE PUDDING (M)

1 pint milk
2 ounces butter, heated

In this boil some fine noodles and cool, add five yolks, beaten, with five tablespoonfuls sugar, one pint sour cream, five whites of eggs, beaten stiff. Bake and serve with wine sauce.*

* Wine Sauce is described in Matzos Pudding recipe.

KUGEL (T)

Soak five wheat rolls in water, then press the bread quite dry. Knead it with three-fourths pound raw suet,* two heaping handfuls brown sugar, one tablespoonful molasses, cinnamon, cloves and lemon, one tablespoonful water, a pinch of salt. Mix very well together. Line an iron pot with alternate layers of above dough and stewed and stoned prunes. Bake two hours; baste often with prune juice.

*Note: This recipe may be treife since suet is not usually kosher.

*The following recipe is written
just as it originally appeared.*

MATZOS PUDDING (F)

3   matzos (soaked, pressed and stirred until smooth),
10   eggs beaten separately,
2   large apples (peeled and grated),
1   cup goose fat,
1/2 cup white wine,
     Grated rind of a lemon,
     Sugar to sweeten,
1/2 teaspoon salt.

Stir one-half hour, and lastly fold in the beaten whites. Grease form well, bake in a moderate oven one-half hour and serve with wine sauce: six eggs, one cup weak wine, sugar to taste. Stir constantly until it thickens as it is apt to curdle.

HOW DID THERE GET TO BE
SO MANY KUGEL RECIPES?

Once upon a time (this is true), in the "Old Country", primarily Eastern Europe and Russia, people did not measure ingredients as they do today. When asked for a recipe by someone who was interested, they would show how the food was prepared and say, as my grandmother did, "you use a little bit of this and a little bit of that", (the Yiddish expression is *sheet a rhine)* or a handful, a dash or a pinch. Bake it in the oven" (no length of time was given). Rough estimates were used and people were remarkably successful in making very tasty dishes.

Although pounds and ounces eventually became used, there were no standard measuring cups and spoons, as we have today. If the use of a spoon or cup was mentioned when giving recipes, my Bubby (grandmother), Gittle Rosenthal Finklestein, always referred to her favorite huge soup spoon or tiny, little teaspoon or her favorite glass that she used for cooking and baking. Some people measured by using egg shells. After cleaning and drying the shells, they used them as measuring devices.

53

Since nobody really knew for sure exactly how much of this or that was to be used, they "guesstimated." The recipes were then altered as they were passed to others, something like whispering down the lane.

Local customs, dietary laws and lack of money throughout history drastically affected the types of food available to the Jews. Food supplies of the Ashkenazic Jews were often very limited since they lived primarily in cold regions. During the Middle Ages, pepper was a popular spice and "Salt and Pepper Kugels" became a favorite.

ASHKENAZIC
SALT AND PEPPER KUGEL (F)

3   cups broad noodles, cooked and drained
3/4 cup chicken fat (schmaltz)
4   eggs, well beaten
    salt and pepper

Preheat oven to 400 degrees.   4 servings

Add to noodles salt and pepper to taste, eggs and fat. Pour into greased casserole dish. Bake until top is well browned, about 45 minutes.

VIENNESE NOODLE PUDDING (M)

8   ounces noodles
1-1/4 cups milk
2   teaspoons plus 3 tablespoons butter
3   eggs, separated
        Salt and freshly ground black pepper to taste

Preheat oven to 350 degrees.   6-8 servings

Break noodles into small pieces and cook in milk until well done. Let them cool but do not drain. Grease an 8 or 9 inch frying pan (with metal handle so it will not melt in oven) with the 2 teaspoons butter. Cream the remaining butter. Add the egg yolks one by one, beating steadily. Add the noodles with the milk. Beat egg whites until stiff but not dry and fold into noodles. Season with salt and pepper to taste. Spread mixture evenly in the greased pan and bake 40-50 minutes or until lightly browned. Cool slightly. Loosen edges and turn out onto a warm plate.

KUGEL AND CHOLENT

Since the Middle Ages in Eastern Europe people have been baking steamed kugel in a round covered earthenware or metal pot in the center or on top of cholent.

Cholent (stew) has been around for at least 2,500 years and was served at the earliest Sabbaths. German Jews called this starchy stew "schalet." Probably as versatile as kugel, every town and every family seemed to have their own favorite ways of preparing cholent.

The ingredients, in many different combinations, would be beans, peas, rice, potatoes and/or barley. Vegetables such as carrots, turnips, green beans and onions are added along with a variety of herbs and spices. Meat or poultry can also be included. The amount of meat one added in early Poland and Russia was a sign of how wealthy the family was.

Sweet kugel became the official noontime Sabbath dessert. By baking it overnight together with cholent, the entire meal would be ready to eat after Saturday morning religious services or at *"schul ende"*, as it would be referred to in Yiddish. The word "cholent" is possibly derived from this expression. Or it may have been taken from the French word *"chaud"* or the Hebrew word *"chamim"*, both meaning "hot."

Since cooking is not permitted on the Sabbath in a very religious home, the cholent-and-kugel was prepared and partially cooked before sundown on Friday. It was then baked overnight on a low flame to prevent it from burning.

To help retain the juices, the meal was covered with either cheesecloth or sealed with a dough made of flour and water. Plenty of water was added to allow for evaporation. Water cannot be added on the Sabbath since that would be considered work.

The pots were taken to the baker who marked them with the owner's name. Young non-Jewish boys would deliver the meals after synagogue. Frequently there were mistakes and the true owner would not get the meal she had prepared. Not to worry -- the other meal was probably wonderful and later recipes were exchanged!

Although work is not permitted on the Sabbath, carrying is allowed within the home. In small villages (shtetls), a wire called the *"Eruv"* was used to enclose the community. This made the village "one household" where carrying was permitted. If the wire broke, the food was passed from house to house until it reached its owner.

BASIC CHOLENT (F)

2   large onions, peeled and sliced or diced
2   tablespoons oil
1/2 lb. dried lima beans, soaked in water until tender
9   medium potatoes, quartered, unpeeled
2   lb. beef cubes
        salt, pepper, paprika, garlic powder to taste
1   bay leaf
1/2 cup catsup
3   carrots, quartered and scrubbed

Coat meat with flour. Brown with onions in oil in bottom of dutch oven, or any heavy pot with tight fitting lid. Add remaining ingredients. Add water to cover and cook over low heat 3-4 hours. Check periodically and add water as needed. Place in oven on lowest setting for overnight cooking, if desired, until noontime. Kugel can be steamed in center of cholent.
6 servings

To keep cholent (or soup) hot for several hours, wrap pot in several blankets. Or place heated cholent in a large towel and put at the end of a bed and cover with quilts. The cholent will stay warm, and so will the bed!

BELIEVE IT OR NOT

The flavor of cholent juices will penetrate the eggs after overnight cooking and the egg shells will become edible.

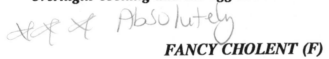

FANCY CHOLENT (F)

```
2-1/2  lbs. beef brisket or top of round well trimmed and
       cut into 6 large chunks
1/3    cup oil
3      cloves garlic, chopped fine
2      medium onions, diced
3      quarts water
1      cup lima beans, uncooked
1/2    cup pearl barley
2      ripe tomatoes, quartered
2      stalks celery, quartered
3      carrots, cut into large chunks, brushed
1/2    teaspoon paprika
1      tablespoon chopped parsley
1      teaspoon salt
1/2    teaspoon pepper
1      bay leaf
       Stuffed derma
2      unbroken eggs, in the shell, washed
```

Preheat oven to 250 degrees.   8 servings

Saute the garlic and onion in vegetable oil. Add
remaining ingredients. Bring to boil on top of stove.
Cover and bake in oven 4-6 hours. Check cholent
periodically to be sure there is enough water. Add 1/2
cup as needed. This can be baked in a large roasting
pan with kugel in round pan in center of cholent. The
edges of kugel pan should be higher than cholent
ingredients. Pan will probably float on top of cholent.

CHOLENT KUGELS

Also see: Steamed Three-Bowl Apple Passover Kugel, p.175

RUMANIAN KUGEL BALLS (P)

1	cup cornmeal
1	cup flour
2	tablespoons sugar
1-1/2	teaspoons salt
1/2	teaspoon paprika
	Freshly ground black pepper
1/2	cup oil
1/2	cup boiling water

Stir all ingredients together. Drop heaping tablespoons
of mixture into cholent covered with bubbling hot
liquid. 6-8 servings

THIS NEEDS SOME GRAVY KUGEL (P)

1/2 cup bread crumbs
2   cups flour
8   ounces kosher shortening
2   eggs
1/2 teaspoon salt
1/2 teaspoon pepper

Preheat oven to 450 degrees.   8 servings

Sprinkle a greased 2-quart casserole dish with bread
crumbs. Combine shortening, flour and eggs. Add salt
and pepper and pour mixture into dish. Cover with heavy
foil and bake 30 minutes. Reduce heat to 375 degrees
and bake two more hours or at 250 degrees four hours in
the center of a cholent.

SUGAR AND SPICE AND EVERYTHING NICE, THAT'S WHAT KUGELS ARE MADE OF

When times were prosperous fruits, vegetables, sugar and spice were added. Sugar and cinnamon have always been favorite additions to foods. Cinnamon has been used extensively in Jewish cuisine since before King Solomon's time. Trade with spice producing countries in the far east had been an important occupation of the Jews until the 20th century. Jews have always had a passion for sugar. It was brought from Asia to Europe in 636 A.C.E. In the 14th century, Jews introduced sugar to the Western world. Today, as it has been for hundreds of years, cinnamon and sugar are used more often than any other spices in kugels. Cottage cheese has been used in Europe for several hundred years. It is made from skim milk and its benefit as a low calorie substitute for meat was recognized after World War I. It is one of the staple food items of a kugel mavin (as well as sour cream and cream cheese, noodles, butter or margarine and other things).

FRUIT AND SPICE KUGEL (P)

8 cups stale bread crumbs
4 tablespoons water
6 tablespoons sweet red wine
2 eggs
2 apples, with skin, diced
2 pears, with skin, diced
6 plums, peeled and diced
1/4 cup raisins
1/2 cup oil
3 tablespoons lemon juice
1 tablespoon lemon rind, grated
1 teaspoon cinnamon
1 teaspoon allspice
1/2 teaspoon clove
1/2 teaspoon salt

Preheat oven to 250 degrees.   10 servings

Sprinkle water and 1/2 of the wine over bread crumbs and
mix well. Combine remaining ingredients and stir into
crumb mixture. Pour into greased 10" baking pan.
Cover, bake overnight in the center of a cholent or in
pan filled halfway with water.

STEAMED PEAR KUGEL (P)

Filling:

3 hard pears, pared and sliced
1/2 cup sugar
1 teaspoon cinnamon
  pinch of nutmeg
  pinch of salt
1/2 cup raisins
4-5 prunes, soaked, pitted and diced

Dough:

1-1/2 cups flour
1/4 teaspoon salt
2 teaspoons baking powder
1 teaspoon sugar
4 tablespoons pareve margarine
2 eggs
  a few tablespoons of water

Mix filling ingredients and set aside. Grease a 2-quart baking dish. Sift the flour, salt, baking powder and sugar together. Add 2 tablespoons of margarine and eggs and work into medium to loose dough with your hands or food processor. Add a little water if too stiff. If too loose to roll, add a little flour (the softer the dough, the better). Knead into round ball. Roll out about 1/8" thick. Spread filling mixture over dough. Dot with remaining margarine. Fold edges in toward center, pinching into the shape of a ball. With a wide spatula, transfer to baking dish. Set dish into center of cholent pan. Surround with cholent ingredients. Or place dish in a pan of hot water making sure water is lower than kugel pan top. Cover kugel tightly and bake 4-5 hours or overnight. As water or cholent liquid evaporates, add more water so that kugel will brown slowly and not burn.

The Jewish Manual, printed in 1846 and anonymously edited by "A Lady", was the first Jewish cookbook printed in English. It contains some of the earliest kugel recipes. The following recipes are from this delightful book and are written here just as they originally appeared. Kugel and Commean is a recipe for a cholent, or stew, baked in a basin (or large pot) with a kugel. It calls for Spanish peas (garbanzos or chick peas), beans, and all-night baking in a baker's oven and possibly serving it with lemon and brandy sauce.

KUGEL AND COMMEAN (F OR T*)

Soak one pint of Spanish peas and one pint of Spanish beans all night in three pints of water; take two marrow bones, a calf's foot, and three pounds of fine gravy-beef, crack the bones and tie them to prevent the marrow escaping, and put all together into a pan; [then take one pound of flour, half a pound of shred suet, a little grated nutmeg and ground ginger, cloves and allspice, one pound of coarse brown sugar, and the crumb of a slice of bread, first soaked in water and pressed dry, mix all these ingredients together into a paste, grease a quart basin and put it in, covering the basin with a plate set in the middle of the pan with the beans, meat, etc.]. Cover the pan lightly down with coarse brown paper, and let it remain all the night and the next day, (until required) in a baker's oven, when done, take out the basin containing the pudding, and skim the fat from the gravy which must be served as soup; the meat, etc., is extremely savory and nutritious, but is not a very seemly dish for table. The pudding must be turned out of the basin, and a sweet sauce flavored with lemon and brandy is a fine addition.

Note: Portion of the above recipe in [] brackets is the kugel -- referred to later in recipe as pudding. Shred suet may not be kosher and therefore this is possibly a treif recipe. It is written exactly as it originally appeared.

The following five recipes are written just as they originally appeared.

DESSERT SAUCE (T)

Mix a table-spoonful of flour, with two of water, add a little wine, lemon peel grated, and a small pit of clarified suet, of the size of a walnut, grated nutmeg, and sugar, put on in a saucepan, stirring one way, and adding water if too thick, lemon juice, or essence of noyeau, or almonds may be substituted to vary the flavour.

A LUCTION OR A RACHAEL (M)

Make a thin nouilles paste, cut into strips of about two inches wide, leave it to dry, then boil the strips in a little water, and drain through a colander; when the water is strained off, mix it with beaten eggs, white sugar, a little fresh butter, and grated lemon peel; bake or boil in a shape lined with preserved cherries, when turned out pour over a fine custard, or cream, flavored with brandy, and sweetened to taste.

EGG PASTE, CALLED IN MODERN COOKERY NOUILLES (P)

This is formed by making a paste of flour and beaten eggs, without either butter or water; it must be rolled out extremely thin and left to dry; it may then be cut into narrow strips or stamped with paste cutters. It is more fashionable in soups than vermicelli.

FANCY CREAMS (M)

Put into a basin a pint of cream, to which add four ounces of powdered white sugar, and the rind of lemon rubbed on a lump of sugar, and a glass of sherry wine; whisk them well and mix with it half an ounce of dissolved isinglass, beat it all thoroughly together, and fill the mould, which should be set in ice till wanted. A table-spoonful of marasquino added to the above, will make "Italian Cream." A table-spoonful of fresh or preserved pine-apple will make "Pine-apple Cream"; this will require the addition of a little lemon syrup. A table-spoonful of ratifia, will make it "Ratifia Cream." The juice of strawberries or raspberries make fine fruit creams; "Mille Fruit Cream" is made by mixing with the cream any kind of small preserved fruit.

A very popular dessert pudding during the 18th century in Great Britain was called "Vermicelli Pudding." The recipe below was taken from a rare book called The English Art of Cookery, According to Present Practice *by Richard Briggs, published in 1788 in Dublin. Many kugel recipes used today have been adapted from this old favorite. It is written here just as it originally appeared.*

18TH CENTURY
VERMICELLI PUDDING (M)

Take a quarter of a pound of vermicelli, and boil it in a pint of milk till it is tender with a flick of cinnamon and a laurel leaf or two; then take out the cinnamon and laurel leaf, and put in half a pint of cream, a quarter of a pound of butter melted, the same weight of sugar, with the yolks of six eggs well beat; lag a puff-pastre round the edge of your dish, put it in, and bake it three quarters of an hour in a moderate oven. For variety, you may add half a pound of currants clean washed and picked.

THE SEPHARDIM

After being deported from ancient Judea (a portion of Israel which includes Jerusalem) Jews established small communities in Europe, India and the Orient. Most of the Oriental Jews or their descendants eventually returned to the Middle East.

The word "Sepharad" means Spain. However, it originally referred to an area in Asia where exiled Jerusalemites went. The Oriental Jews never lived in the Iberian Peninsula (Spain) or any other part of Europe. But they are referred to as Sephardim, just as the Spanish Jews are.

After the Spanish Inquisition, in 1492, most of the Spanish Jews went eastward to the Balkans and central areas of the Ottoman Turkish Empire. Many settled in the Northern coast of Africa, primarily Morocco. Others went to Italy and Middle Eastern areas. Later, Holland, major cities in Europe and both North and South America became homelands.

Ladino or Judeo-Spanish, which is also known as Judezmo, is the "folk" language of the Spanish Sephardim. It is written in Hebrew letters, just as Yiddish is. It is basically Castilian Spanish with some Hebrew mixed in. Words of local languages are also part of Ladino, particularly Turkish.

Sephardim have many names for kugel; one is *"pyota."* In Israel, kugel is also called *"pashtida"* (another name too for potato pancakes). Their kugels have ingredients such as farina, eggplant, and barley. They generally use a wider variety of herbs and spices than Ashkenazic cooks. Layered kugels are said to be of Sephardic origin.

ISRAELI THEME PARTY

Have an Israeli theme party and serve the Eggplant Kugel, Middle Eastern Farina Kugel, Bulgur and Nut Kugel, and Jerusalem or Sweet and Hot Kugel with Hummus, Tabouleh, Tahini Dip, and Eggplant Salad. These dips are Middle Eastern or Mediterranean in origin and are very popular in Israel.

PYOTA GREEK STYLE FARINA KUGEL (M)

3-1/2 cups boiling water
2/3   cup quick Cream of Wheat cereal (farina)*
1   cup instant nonfat dry milk powder
2   tablespoons butter, small pieces
1/2   cup sugar
1/3   cup honey
1/2   teaspoon vanilla extract
1/4   teaspoon cinnamon
5   eggs

<u>Topping (optional)</u>: Fresh fruit

Preheat oven to 325 degrees.   10 servings

Stir cereal and milk powder into boiling water and immediately lower the heat to medium. Cook cereal stirring continuously until thick. Remove from heat and add butter, sugar, honey, vanilla and cinnamon. While beating eggs, add one cup of cereal mixture. Stir egg mixture into rest of cereal mixture. Pour into greased 10" x 10" pan and sprinkle top with cinnamon. Bake one hour or until knife inserted comes out clean. Serve cold topped with fresh fruit if desired.

*You can substitute grits for a Southern American flair.

MIDDLE EASTERN FARINA KUGEL (P)

Tastes like Matzah Meal Pancakes. Puffy like a souffle.

```
1/2 cup farina (Cream of Wheat)
2   cups boiling water
1   tablespoon pareve margarine
1/2 cup sugar
1/2 teaspoon salt
1   teaspoon grated lemon rind
5   eggs, separated
```

Preheat oven to 350 degrees.   10 servings

Add farina to boiling water. Lower heat, add margarine, sugar, and salt and cook for 5 minutes. Remove from heat and let cool. Beat egg whites until stiff. Mix lemon rind and egg yolks into farina mixture. Fold in whites. Grease a 10" x 10" pan and pour in mixture. Bake 30 minutes.

EGGPLANT KUGEL (P)

```
1   large eggplant, pared and sliced
4   tablespoons pareve margarine
1   onion, chopped
1   green pepper, chopped
    salt and pepper to taste
2   small eggs, slightly beaten
1/2 to 1 cup cracker crumbs or matzah meal
2   tablespoons margarine, melted
paprika
```

Preheat oven to 350 degrees.   Serves 6-8

Cook eggplant in water until tender (20 minutes). Drain and mash. Saute pepper and onion in margarine until tender. Mix together with eggplant, eggs, salt and pepper and crumbs. Pour into a greased 8" pan. Top with melted margarine and sprinkle with paprika. Bake 45 minutes until browned.

JERUSALEM KUGEL (P) *& try hot*

This spicy kugel which combines Ashkenazic and Sephardic cooking styles, is very popular in Jerusalem, particularly among Hassidic Jews. After being baked in a slow oven overnight, it is served to dignitaries, at important events and celebrations and on the Sabbath after Saturday morning services. The women of Mea Shearim make this kugel in huge quantities and sell it.

```
12   ounces fine noodles, parboiled and drained
1/2  cup oil
1/4  cup sugar
3    medium eggs, beaten
2    teaspoons black pepper
1 teaspoon salt
```

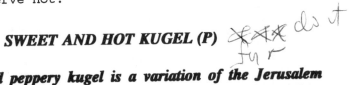 *change temperature*

Preheat oven to 175 degrees.   8 servings

Pour 1/4 cup oil over cooked noodles and keep warm. Add sugar to the remaining 1/4 cup of oil and heat over a low flame. Gently shake pan occasionally while cooking but do not stir. Cook for about 20 minutes until sugar caramelizes and turns dark brown. As soon as the sugar is ready, slowly pour it over the warm noodles. Mix thoroughly. Add eggs, salt and pepper. Pour into greased 8" x 8" pan. Cover and bake overnight or up to 14 hours. Serve hot.

SWEET AND HOT KUGEL (P) *do it try*

This sweet and peppery kugel is a variation of the Jerusalem Kugel. In 1989 I brought it to the world premiere of the show entitled "Sweet and Hot in Harlem", a spectacular review of Harold Arlen's music. My cousin, Robert Cohen, was the producer. The cast liked the kugel so much that I had to bake it for them again when they appeared in Buffalo, N. Y. in 1991.

```
1      lb. thin spaghetti, broken, cooked and drained
1/2    lb. pareve margarine
1      cup brown sugar
6      eggs, beaten
2-1/2  teaspoons black pepper
1      teaspoon salt
```

Preheat oven to 350 degrees.   10 servings

Cook margarine and sugar in a large pan stirring
continuously for 5 minutes until sugar begins to
caramelize. Add spaghetti immediately. Add eggs, salt
and pepper. Pour into lightly greased 10" x 10" pan.
Bake one hour.

BULGUR AND NUT KUGEL (P)

2   cups bulgur
5   cups water
1/2-1 cup sugar
2   eggs, well beaten
1/4 cup honey
2   cups ground walnuts or almonds
1   tablespoon cinnamon
1/2 teaspoon light salt

Preheat oven to 350 degrees.   10 servings

Boil bulgur in water. Reduce heat and simmer, stirring
frequently for 30 minutes. Add remaining ingredients
and mix well. Pour into greased 10" x 10" baking pan
Bake 40 minutes.

EGGPLANT SALAD (P)

2   tablespoons olive oil
1   small onion, finely chopped
1   clove garlic, minced
1/2   green bell pepper
1   cup fresh mushrooms, chopped
1   medium eggplant, unpeeled, chopped
1/4   cup black olives, pitted and chopped
1-1/4 tablespoons red wine vinegar
1/3   cup dry wine
1/2   teaspoon sugar
1/4   teaspoon oregano
1/2   teaspoon salt
1/4   teaspoon fresh ground black pepper
2   tablespoons pine nuts

Saute onion, garlic, and green pepper in oil until
tender. Add mushrooms and eggplant. Cover pan and
simmer, stirring often until eggplant is very soft. Add
remaining ingredients; continue to cook for about 20
more minutes until everything is nicely blended. Allow
mixture to cool and serve with thin-sliced french bread.

HUMMUS (P)

1   cup prepared chickpeas, drained
     (reserve 2 tablespoons of liquid)
3   cloves fresh garlic, minced
1/4 cup lemon juice
1/4 cup "tahini" sesame paste
1   teaspoon olive oil
pinch of salt and white pepper

Mince garlic in a food processor. Add chickpeas, lemon juice, tahini (which has been thoroughly stirred), salt and pepper and reserved chickpea liquid. Blend to a pastelike consistency. Add olive oil to make mixture spreadable. Serve with pita bread that has been cut into triangles for dipping.

TAHINI DIP (P)

1/2   cup "tahini" sesame paste
1/2   cup water
1/4   teaspoon salt
2-1/2 tablespoons lemon juice
3   cloves of garlic
pinch of white pepper

Stir tahini and add water, salt, lemon juice, garlic and pepper. Add more water if a thinner consistency is desired. Garnish with paprika and fresh parsley. Serve with pita bread that has been cut into triangles for dipping.

TABOULEH (P)

1-1/2 cups bulgur
4   medium ripe tomatoes
1   cup fresh chopped parsley
1   cup chopped scallions
1/2   cup olive oil
1/2   cup fresh lemon juice
1   teaspoon salt
2   tablespoons dried mint, crumbled

Pour bulgur into a sieve. Dip filled sieve into water to cover bulgur. Lift sieve and squeeze out excess water. Stir in remaining ingredients. Cover and refrigerate overnight. Stir salad during refrigeration period and just before serving. Bulgur will soften and the flavors of the salad will blend together. Serve with pita bread that has been cut into triangles.

MENU

FRIDAY NIGHT SABBATH OR HOLIDAY MEAL

1st Course

Gefilte fish with horseradish or
Chopped liver

2nd Course

Chicken soup with matzah balls,
noodles or kreplach

3rd Course

Chicken or Brisket
Potato kugel or other pareve kugel
Glazed carrots or green vegetable
Cucumber or Tomato and Green Pepper Salad
Challah (egg bread) -- Matzah during Passover
Traditional Sweet Wine

4th Course

Fruit
Dessert Kugel
Coffee or tea

SATURDAY NOON MEAL

Fruit salad
Cholent
Cholent Kugel

I have integrated Ashkenazic and Sephardic cooking styles into the Friday Night Sabbath or Holiday menu. After all — kugels are not just from one part of the world, so why should the menu be limited?

1ST COURSE

Gefilte fish or chopped liver is frequently served in Ashkenazic Jewish homes on the Sabbath and at holiday-time. Rabbinic Jewish authorities determined that removing bones from a fish in a certain way was work. Since no work may be done on the Sabbath, people started making fish that was boned and gefilte fish became popular. It is frequently seen·in Polish restaurants where it is listed on the menus as "fish, Jewish style."

Carp and whitefish are frequently used in recipes but almost any firm fish can be used. The head and bones of the fish are sometimes cooked in the broth along with the formed fish mixture. It is usually served cold in small ball shapes for snacks or in larger ovals as an appetizer over a lettuce leaf and topped with a cooked carrot slice. Ground horseradish that is colored with beet juice, known as red horseradish, usually accompanies it. Some people serve gefilte fish with the jellied stock, but I never liked it.

Gefilte fish can be found in jars in the ethnic foods section in many grocery stores throughout North America or you can use the recipe below.

try

GEFILTE FISH (P)

3	pounds haddock fillets, or similar firm fish
2	medium onions
2	large carrots
3	medium eggs
1-1/2	teaspoons lite salt
3/4	teaspoon freshly ground black pepper
3/4	teaspoon sugar
3/4	cup matzah meal

In a food processor chop fish, carrots and onions with steel blade. Add egg, salt, pepper, sugar and matzah meal; process until smooth. With wet hands, form mixture into balls, either bite-size or into fat oval-shaped patties.

Broth:

8	cups water
4	stalks celery
2	onions
3	large carrots
3	pareve bouillon cubes
1/2	tablespoon freshly ground pepper
1	tablespoon sugar

Place broth ingredients into a large, deep pot and cover. Bring to a boil and then reduce to a simmer. Stir to be sure bouillon cubes have dissolved. Carefully slide the formed fish into water. Cook slowly for one hour if bite-size or two hours for larger pieces occasionally turning fish with a spoon. Allow to cool in the pot and carefully remove the patties with a slotted spoon. After the fish has been removed, strain off the vegetables and loose pieces of fish. This stock should jell when chilled. However, if it does not, add a package of kosher unflavored gelatin. Serve warm or chilled fish with jellied fish stock (if desired), horseradish and a carrot slice from broth. Makes 10-12 patties.

yes try

QUICK GEFILTE FISH (P)

4 pieces jarred gefilte fish, any brand
1 small onion
1 small carrot, sliced thin
1 stalk celery, diced
dash of ground pepper
1 teaspoon paprika

Drain jellied stock from jar into a pot. Add onion, carrot, celery, pepper and paprika. Cover and bring to a boil. Simmer for 10-15 minutes, until vegetables are soft. Add fish and simmer 15 minutes, covered. Serve warm or chilled fish with jellied fish stock (if desired), horseradish and a carrot slice from broth.

yes mb try

CHOPPED LIVER (F)

1 pound liver, chicken or beef
1 or 2 tablespoons oil
1 large yellow onion
2 large eggs, hard boiled
1/2 cup light mayonnaise
salt and pepper to taste

In a food processor, chop the onion. Brown onion in hot oil and remove from heat. Wash liver and broil until it is not pink inside but do not overcook. Cut liver into chunks and chop using steel blade in food processor or meat grinder to a course meal texture. Add hard-boiled eggs, onions, mayonnaise, salt and pepper. Mix thoroughly and serve.

Serving suggestion: Serve with tomatoes, chopped onion and crackers or bread.

2ND COURSE

Mother knows best!

Chicken soup has been referred to as "Jewish Penicillin" for generations. Scientists finally decided to check it out. They found there really is something in chicken soup that makes it very effective to help relieve symptoms of colds and flu.

MOTHER'S CHICKEN SOUP (F)

```
1    whole chicken, cut up
1    whole onion, peeled
3    stalks celery, with leaves
2 or 3 large carrots, brushed
1    tablespoon lite salt
1/2 teaspoon white (cayenne) pepper
kosher chicken bouillon cubes, as needed**
```

Place chicken into a large pot filled about half way with water, covering washed chicken. Bring water to a boil and "skim the scum", as my mother would say, with a spoon. Cut washed and brushed carrots into one inch chunks. Thoroughly wash celery and break each stalk in half. Reduce heat to simmer and place vegetables, salt and pepper into pot. Cover pot and continue to cook for two or three hours. Taste soup to make sure it is flavorful enough. If not, add one bouillon cube at a time until you obtain the taste you desire. Place a colander over a large container and pour soup into it to strain. Separate the chicken from vegetables. Remove skin and bones from chicken. Pour chicken, carrots and broth back into cleaned pot, heat and serve. Add noodles*, kreplach, mandlen or matzah balls.

* See "Noodle Kugel Chapter" for Homemade Noodles.

To remove fat from soup:

Put chicken and carrots in one container and broth in another. Refrigerator overnight and the fat will solidify at the top of the now jellied broth. Take it away!

** *To tell the truth, my mother never used the bouillon cubes. Occasionally the soup would come out a little watery tasting, especially if she tried to stretch the soup by adding more water. My husband used to call it "duty chicken soup." That is an expression the sailors used when he was in the Navy. He said, "They used to have a duty chicken that was always on call. When it came time to prepare the chicken soup, they waved a chicken through the soup a few times and then put it away until the next time they had to make soup."*

Many cultures have similar foods and kreplach is one of them. This is a filled noodle that is popular in Ashkenazic Jewish cuisine. It is believed to have been adapted from the Chinese wanton or Italian ravioli. The Polish version is a pirogi. My grandmother, I called her Bubby, who came to America from Russia in the late 1800's, used to make kreplach stuffed with ground chicken and she served it in chicken soup. Some people like to fry it and serve it with gravy.

KREPLACH (F)

```
1       tablespoon oil
1       small onion, chopped
1-1/2 cups chicken, cooked and finely shredded
1       egg, beaten
1       tablespoon chopped parsley
salt and pepper to taste
Homemade Noodle Dough recipe
```

Lightly brown the onion in oil. Finely grind chicken in food processor. Add onions, beaten egg, parsley and salt and pepper. Divide the dough into two balls. Cover with a moist towel. Quickly roll out half of the dough with a rolling pin or through a pasta machine as directed in Homemade Noodle Dough recipe until thin and easy to handle. Cut into strips that are 2 inches wide. Put 1/2 teaspoon mounds of filling about 2 inches apart and cut into 2 inch squares. Fold into a triangle and press edges together. Wet inside edges if necessary to make them stick. Place each kreplach on a floured piece of wax paper until you are ready to cook. Place into boiling water and cook 10-15 minutes. Kreplach will rise to the top of the pot as they are cooking. Uncooked kreplach can be covered and refrigerated for one day. They can also be frozen. Makes 50-60

Absolutely absolutely

MATZAH BALLS (KNAIDLACH) (P OR F)

```
1    cup matzah meal
1/2  cup water or club soda (seltzer)
4    eggs
1/3  cup oil
1    teaspoon salt
dash pepper
```

Beat eggs and add water, oil, salt and pepper. Mix well. Add matzah meal and stir thoroughly. Refrigerate one hour. Form into 1-1/2 inch balls and gently drop into soup with a spatula or large spoon. Cover pot with lid and do not remove lid of pot while cooking. Cook 20 minutes.

VARIATIONS:

Use: 1/2 cup chicken soup instead of water. Matzah balls will come out heavier.

Add: dash of garlic powder, ginger, cinnamon
  or 2 tablespoons finely chopped parsley
  or 1 tbsp. finely chopped nuts plus a dash ginger
  or 1 cup of mashed potatoes
  or 3 grated and well drained raw potatoes plus
      1 cup of mashed potatoes

Add "soul" or neshomas by combining:

```
      2 tablespoons matzah meal
      2 tablespoons hot fat
      1 egg
      dash of salt
```

Tuck a small ball of this mixture in the center of each knaidle or dumpling.

  or put chopped grebenes or chopped liver or a combination of both in the center

  or tuck in a few slivered almonds

MANDLEN (P)

1   cup flour, unbleached and presifted
1/4 teaspoon salt
1/2 teaspoon baking powder
2   eggs
1   tablespoon oil

Preheat oven to 375 degrees.
Beat together eggs and oil. Slowly add to flour and
knead until smooth. Roll to 1/4 inch thickness and cut
into 1/2 inch pieces. Place on greased cookie sheet and
bake 15 minutes.

*Every year at the Jewish Community Center of Central Florida
in Maitland (north of Orlando) during their Hanukkah festival,
there is a Chicken Soup and Kugel Kontest. Here is the 1992
winning chicken soup recipe. Award Winning Kugel recipe is on
p. 84*

AWARD WINNING CHICKEN SOUP RECIPE (F)
by Sophie Marcus Treibwasser

3 lb. chicken, cut in quarters
2 carrots, sliced
1 large onion, sliced
2 stalks of celery with leaves, sliced
1 large parsnip, sliced
1 tablespoon chopped parsley, dried or fresh
1 teaspoon dill, dried or fresh
1 kosher chicken bouillon cube
1 kosher beef bouillon cube

Remove skin from chicken and place into a pressure
cooker or large pot. Add carrots, onion, celery,
parsnip, bouillon cubes, parsley and dill. Cover with
water and cook until vegetables are soft (15 minutes if
you are using pressure cooker). Drain broth into
another pot. Remove chicken and   all bones. Place
cooked vegetables and one cup of soup into a blender or
food processor with steel blade. Blend until pureed.
Add soup and heat. Serve with crackers and boiled
chicken.

3RD COURSE

A meal should look as attractive on a plate as it is tasty and well balanced. I like to serve a colorful meal with something red or orange and green. If it includes oranges or red peppers I might accompany it with fresh steamed asparagus, broccoli, or whole green beans and a kugel that is not sweet.

ISRAELI CHICKEN WITH OLIVES AND ORANGES (F)

```
3    lbs. chicken parts
2    tablespoons lemon juice
2    tablespoons honey
2    cups orange juice
1    tablespoon grated orange peel
1/2  teaspoon salt
1/2  teaspoon paprika
1/4  teaspoon ginger
1/4  teaspoon nutmeg
1/4  teaspoon cumin
1/4  teaspoon cinnamon
2    tablespoons cornstarch
1/2  cup pitted black olives, sliced
1    large can mandarin oranges, drained
```

Preheat oven to 350 degrees.   Serves 4

Bake chicken in a covered 9" x 13" pan 30 minutes. Stir together honey and lemon juice in a saucepan over a medium heat. Add 1 cup of orange juice and spices and heat to boiling. Dissolve cornstarch in remaining orange juice and add to mixture in saucepan. Reduce heat and simmer, stirring constantly until mixture thickens. Pour over chicken and bake another 15 minutes. Place on a serving dish and pour on sauce. Garnish with olives and oranges.

Garnishes such as fresh fruit slices and snipped parsley perk up a meal that might otherwise be just brown and white. A potato kugel and carrots with grapes would be good with this dish.

CHICKEN IN WINE (F)

```
3 lbs. boneless chicken breast
dash of salt and pepper
2       cups flour
3       tablespoons margarine
1       tablespoon oil
1       cup Marsala or Madeira wine
1       cup kosher chicken stock
1/2     lb. fresh mushrooms
fresh snipped parsley
```

Pound thin filets of chicken between two pieces of waxed paper. Add salt and pepper to flour and lightly coat washed chicken. Melt margarine in skillet with oil and saute chicken several minutes on each side over moderate heat. Remove chicken and pour off fat. Add wine and chicken stock and bring to boil. Return chicken and add fresh mushrooms. Cover and cook about 20 minutes. Transfer chicken to warm serving dish. Boil sauce a few minutes and pour over chicken. Sprinkle with parsley and serve with potato kugel. Serves 4-6

BRISKET (F)

```
4       pounds brisket
3       tablespoons oil
3       onions, diced or sliced
2       cloves garlic, minced
2       carrots, shredded
2       stalks celery, diced
2       teaspoons salt
1/2     teaspoon paprika
4       bay leaves
1/2     teaspoon fresh ground pepper
1-1/2   cups tomato juice or beef stock
2       tablespoons brown sugar
```

Braise meat on all sides in heated oil in a heavy pot. Add remaining ingredients. Cover and simmer 1-1/2 to 2 hours. Serve hot with its gravy and a pareve broccoli kugel. Serves 6.

CARROTS WITH GRAPES (P)

1   lb. baby carrots
1   teaspoon salt
5   tablespoons brown sugar
1   tablespoon white sugar
3   tablespoons pareve margarine
1/2 cup orange juice
1   cup seedless grapes

Cover carrots with salted water and add one tablespoon each of brown and white sugar. Cook until barely tender, about 25 minutes. Drain liquid. Melt butter and remaining sugar in saucepan. Add orange juice and bring to boil. Add carrots and cook until lightly glazed. Add grapes and cook until warm and serve.

CHALLAH

My husband and I bought our first house about 20 years ago in a small town outside of Haddonfield, N. J. called Barrington. In our neighborhood lived a woman from Morocco who used to make, with other members of her family, challah for Friday night. She sold it and put her sons through college on the money she earned.

This challah was unlike anything I had ever tasted before and it was absolutely the best. Although saffron is frequently used in the preparation of challah, anise seeds give this recipe a special flavor.

Challah is traditionally served at the Friday night Sabbath meal. The bread is usually braided for the Sabbath. The humps at the tops of the bread symbolize the 12 tribes of Israel.

For Rosh Hashanah, challah is usually circular in shape to symbolize a long span of life. The spiral is higher in the center representing the ascent to heaven. "God judges those who will descend and ascend." Sometimes a ladder is formed at the top or a crown to glorify God.

An observant baker will take a one- or two-inch ball of the unbaked dough and burn it or place it in a napkin and throw it away. The Torah says that a small piece of the dough from each large batch of bread must be separated and "offered" to the kohanim (priests) of the Holy Temple. When this is done, a special prayer is said.

MOROCCAN CHALLAH (P)

12   cups unbleached flour
1/2 cup sugar
4   eggs, beaten
1/2 cup oil
1   teaspoon salt

1 tablespoon sesame seeds
1 tablespoon anise seeds
2 packs fresh yeast
3 cups warm water

Preheat oven to 400 degrees.

Pour flour into a large bowl and make a well in the center. Add sugar, 3 eggs, oil, salt, sesame and anise seeds. Pour the yeast into 1/4 cup of warm water with 1 teaspoon of sugar. Let this sit for about 10 minutes until it becomes foamy. Pour yeast into the well.

Work the flour into the ingredients in well. Add more warm water, as needed, about 2 cups. With clean hands, knead the dough on a lightly floured board for about 20 minutes until smooth, elastic and manageable. Be careful not to add too much flour, you do not want dough to be too stiff. Add 1 tablespoon of flour at a time if dough is too sticky.

Oil a large bowl and place dough into it. Turn dough so that top is oiled. Cover bowl with a towel. If it is a very dry day or if you live in a particularly dry area, dampen the towel slightly with warm water. Set the bowl in a warm area near a dryer or over a refrigerator but not on or in a heated oven. Let the dough rise until doubled in size (should take about 30-40 minutes). Punch down and knead once more.

Divide the dough into five pieces. Take a long piece and spiral, making the center higher than the rest of the dough. Repeat with other pieces or braid strips making sure you pinch together ends. Cover for about one hour and let rise until doubled.

Place on greased baking sheet. Brush with remaining egg and a tablespoon of oil and bake 35-45 minutes. Bread should be firm on top and bottom, and should sound hollow when tapped on bottom.

CUCUMBER SALAD (P)

2   cucumbers, peeled and thinly sliced
1   medium onion, peeled and thinly sliced
1/4 cup sugar or sugar substitute equivalent
1/4 cup vinegar
1/2 cup water
1/8 cup oil
1/4 teaspoon each garlic powder and oregano
salt and fresh ground pepper to taste

Place cucumber and onion in a bowl. Mix sugar, vinegar, water and oil in a container with a lid. Shake until thoroughly mixed. Add garlic, oregano, salt and pepper and shake again. Pour over vegetables and marinate in refrigerator overnight.

TOMATO AND GREEN PEPPER SALAD (P)

2 tomatoes, cut into wedges and then halves
2 scallions, chopped
2 green peppers, diced
1/4 cup sugar or sugar substitute equivalent
1/4 cup vinegar
1/2 cup water
1/8 cup oil
1/4 teaspoon each garlic powder and oregano
salt and fresh ground pepper to taste

Place tomatoes, scallions and green pepper in a bowl. Mix sugar, vinegar, water and oil in a container with a lid. Shake until thoroughly mixed. Add garlic, oregano, salt and pepper and shake again. Pour over vegetables and marinate in refrigerator overnight.

Variation: Combine the Cucumber Salad with the Tomato and Green Pepper Salad (the dressing is the same!)

4TH COURSE

AWARD WINNING KUGEL RECIPE (P) ✡
by Mort Lynn

```
8   oz. wide noodles, cooked and drained
2   medium apples (any kind, delicious are fine), peeled
and        cut into 1 inch long by 1/4 inch cubes
1/2 cup white raisins
1/2 cup dried apricots, diced
1/2 cup prunes, diced
6   tablespoons sugar
9   tablespoons oil
4   eggs, beaten
```

Preheat oven to 350 degrees.   20 servings

Mix all ingredients together and pour into a well oiled
9" x 13" pan. Sprinkle with cinnamon and sugar. Bake
40 minutes.

·III·
NOODLE KUGELS

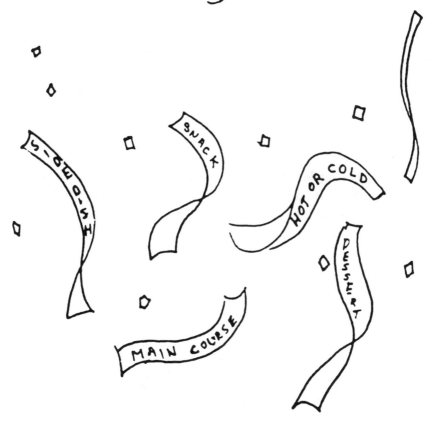

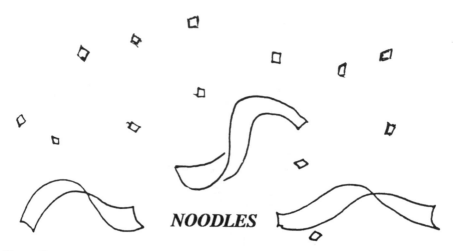

NOODLES

Just about every country in the world has its own form of noodle. Today there are more than 300 different types. However, only a few are used in kugels -- primarily fine, medium, broad and vermicelli noodles. In addition, spinach and whole wheat are used for a healthier twist. The packaged egg or plain varieties are fine to use as is no-yolk but fresh or homemade noodles are even better. The use of elbow macaroni in a kugel, I feel, is stretching the definition of a kugel too far. Let macaroni and cheese continue to be just that with it's famous elbow noodle and let lasagna be lasagna.

NOODLES USED IN KUGELS....

are usually about 2 inches long, however, orzo, spaghetti or fettucini are also sometimes used.

Thin or fine noodles = 1/16 inch wide
Medium noodles   = 1/4 inch wide
Wide noodles   = 1/2 inch wide
Broad noodle   = 1 inch wide

HOMEMADE NOODLE DOUGH (P)

3   large eggs, beaten
3/4 teaspoon salt
2   tablespoons water
2   cups flour, unbleached and presifted

Add salt to eggs and enough flour to make a medium soft dough. Knead well by hand or in food processor. Divide dough into two or three balls and cover with a moist towel. Roll dough to a thin but easy to handle thickness. Cut as desired. Or process floured, hand flattened dough through the rollers of a pasta machine at widest setting. Fold dough two or three times, flatten and put through rollers again. Repeat several times until dough is smooth. Adjust machine to the next setting and put through rollers until smooth. Repeat until you get down to the next to the last setting. Cut dough into desired size noodles.

DAIRY NOODLE KUGELS

The pareve noodle kugels of the Central and Eastern European Jews (Ashkenazim) were adapted by the Middle Eastern Sephardim. From their cheese latkes evolved cheese kugels. It was the Sephardim who introduced cheese and a wide variety of spices to the world of kugel baking. American Jews who's ancestors were either Sephardic or Ashkenazic have become especially creative in embellishing their kugels.

Dairy noodle kugels are the most popular kugels and they are definitely my personal favorites!

SWEET DAIRY NOODLE KUGELS

Also See: A Luction or A Rachel, p. 62
          Cool Whip Jygunda Kugel, p. 39
          18th Century Vermicelli Pudding, p. 63
          Noodle Pudding, p. 52

LUSCIOUS KUGEL (M)

3/4 lb. fine noodles, cooked and drained
4   eggs, beaten
1   cup sugar
1   teaspoon vanilla
1/2 lb. cream cheese
1   cup warm milk
1   cup sour cream
1/4 lb. melted margarine

Preheat oven to 325 degrees.   20 Servings

Combine first four ingredients. Melt cream cheese in warm milk and add sour cream, then melted margarine. Combine with noodle mixture and pour into greased 9" x 13" pan. Bake one hour. Top will be golden.

YELLIN FAMILY KUGEL (M)

1/2 lb. medium noodles, cooked and drained
1/4 lb. margarine or butter, melted
6   eggs, separated
1   pint creamed cottage cheese
6   ounces cream cheese, room temperature
1/4 cup sour cream
1/2 cup sugar

Topping: (optional)

2/3 cup graham cracker crumbs
1/3 cup sugar
1/2 stick butter or margarine, melted and cooled

use Wiet's recipe

Preheat oven to 350 degrees.   20 servings

Prepare topping first by mixing graham cracker crumbs, sugar and melted and cooled butter together and set aside. Mix noodles with stick of melted butter. Cream egg yolks and cream cheese together until fluffy. Add cottage cheese, sour cream and 1/2 cup sugar. Continue beating until well combined. Scrape sides of bowl often. Mix egg yolk mixture with noodles. Beat egg whites until stiff peaks form. Fold into noodle mixture using a cutting and upward motion. Grease a 9" x 13" baking pan and pour in noodle mixture. Crumble graham cracker crumb mixture evenly on top of noodles. Bake one hour. If top is not crispy enough, bake a little longer. Serve hot.

Absolutely

PROUD COW KUGEL (M)

1/2	lb. medium wide noodles, cooked and drained
1/2	lb. farmer cheese
1/2	lb. cottage cheese
1/2	quart milk
1/2	pint sour cream
1/2	teaspoon salt
1-1/2	teaspoons vanilla extract
1/2	dozen eggs, beaten
1/2	cup sugar
1/2	dozen tablespoons melted butter or margarine

Topping:

1/2 cup slivered almonds
1/2 plus 1/4 cup brown sugar

Preheat oven to 350 degrees.   20 servings

Blend together farmer cheese, cottage cheese and sour cream. Add remaining ingredients. Pour mixture into greased spring form pan or 9" x 13" baking pan. Bake 1/2 hour. Remove from oven and sprinkle with topping. Bake another hour. If not firm, bake an additional 10 minutes.

CREAMY KUGEL (M)

```
1/2  stick butter or margarine
1    cup cottage cheese
1    cup sour cream
4    ounces cream cheese
1    lb. medium noodles, cooked and drained
1/2  cup raisins
3/4  cup sugar
6    eggs
```

Preheat oven to 350 degrees.   20 servings

Blend eggs and cream cheese together until smooth. Add
the remaining ingredients. Pour into greased 9" x 13"
pan.

Topping for Creamy Kugel:

use Weits's recipe.

```
1    cup graham cracker crumbs
1/4  cup sugar
1/2  stick margarine
```

Melt margarine and mix with sugar and crumbs. Sprinkle
on top of kugel mixture. Bake 1/2 hour.

TWO CHEESE KUGEL (M)

```
1/2  lb. thin noodles, cooked and drained
6    eggs
2    lbs. cottage cheese
8    ounces cream cheese
1    cup sugar
1/2  stick butter or margarine, melted
1    teaspoon vanilla extract
```

Preheat oven to 350 degrees.   20 servings

Beat cheeses until smooth; add beaten eggs, sugar and
vanilla. Add cooked noodles; blend thoroughly. Pour
melted butter into noodle mixture and stir. Pour into
greased 9" x 13" baking pan. Bake 45 minutes until
lightly browned.

MILCHIDIK KUGEL (M)

```
1      lb. fine noodles, cooked and drained
1/4    lb. margarine, melted
8      ounces cream cheese
1-1/4  lbs. low fat cottage cheese
1      lb. sour cream
1/2    cup milk
6      eggs, beaten
2      teaspoons vanilla extract
1      cup sugar
```

Preheat oven to 350 degrees.   20 servings

Combine all ingredients. Pour into greased 9" x 13" pan. Sprinkle top with either graham cracker crumbs, cinnamon and sugar or prepared fruit topping. Bake one hour or until set.

SIMPLE DAIRY KUGEL (M)

```
1    lb. medium noodles, cooked and drained
6    eggs
8    ounces cream cheese
1    pint sour cream
1/2  cup sugar
1    teaspoon vanilla extract
```

Preheat oven to 350 degrees.   20 servings

Beat eggs well. Add cream cheese, sour cream, sugar and vanilla. Mix thoroughly and add to noodles. Pour into greased 9" x 13" pan. Sprinkle with cinnamon and sugar. Bake one hour.

COTTAGE CHEESE NOODLE PUDDING SOUFFLE (M)

```
1/2 lb. medium noodles, cooked and drained
1/4 lb. butter, softened
1/2 cup sugar
1/2 pint cottage cheese
1   pint dairy sour cream
1/2 teaspoon salt
2   teaspoons vanilla extract
5   eggs
    cinnamon
```

Preheat oven to 350 degrees.   20 servings

Grease a 9" x 13" pan and set aside. In a large bowl,
beat butter and sugar. Add cottage cheese, sour cream,
salt and vanilla. Mix in eggs one at a time, beating
after each addition. Stir in cooked noodles. Pour into
prepared baking dish. Sprinkle top with cinnamon. Bake
50 minutes to one hour until golden brown. Let stand 5
minutes before cutting into squares.

DON'T COOK THE NOODLES KUGEL (M)

1/2   lb. medium noodles, uncooked
8   ounces cream cheese
8   ounces sour cream
8   ounces cottage cheese
      pinch salt
1-1/2 cups milk
1/4   lb. butter or margarine
1/4   cup sugar
4   eggs, beaten

Preheat oven to 325 degrees.   20 servings

Butter 9" x 13" pan. Cover with dry noodles. Put the
rest of ingredients in blender and mix well. Pour over
noodles. Bake 45-55 minutes.

FROSTED FLAKE TOPPED KUGEL (M)

1   lb. medium or wide noodles, cooked and drained
1/2 lb. margarine (save 4 tablespoons)
1   cup sugar
6   eggs   3/4 lb. cream cheese
1   teaspoon vanilla extract   1   pint sour cream
2   cups crushed frosted flakes

Preheat oven to 325 degrees.   20 servings

Beat eggs and sour cream. Add sugar, vanilla and melted
margarine. Add mashed cream cheese and beat well. Mix
with cooked noodles and pour into greased 9" x 13" pan.
Mix frosted flakes with remaining margarine and sprinkle
over kugel. Cover with foil and refrigerate overnight.
Bake one hour until set.

 ## LEMON KUGEL (M)

Prepare same as frosted flake kugel but use corn flakes
and just 1/4 lb. margarine. Add to kugel ingredients
1/3 cup lemon juice and 2 tablespoons lemon rind,
grated.

92

★★ try★5

VIVIAN'S DAIRY NOODLE KUGEL (M)

12 ounces medium or large egg noodles
5 eggs, beaten   1 teaspoon vanilla extract
1/2 lb. cottage cheese   1/2 cup sugar
1/2 lb. cream cheese   1 teaspoon salt
1/4 lb. margarine   8 ounces milk
1 pint sour cream

Topping for Vivian's Dairy Noodle Kugel:

1/4 lb. butter, melted   sugar and cinnamon
2 cups crushed corn flakes

Preheat oven to 350 degrees.   20 servings

Cook and drain noodles. Mix together everything except noodles and topping ingredients in mixer 3-5 minutes. Add noodles and pour into greased 9" x 13" pan. Top with corn flake mixture. Bake one hour.

★★★ ye

ANOTHER WAY TO MAKE IT KUGEL (M) ✡

1/2 lb. medium noodles
4 eggs
1 cup sugar
1 teaspoon vanilla extract
1/4 lb. butter or margarine, melted
12 ounces dry cottage cheese
1/2 lb. cream cheese, room temperature
1 pint sour cream
1 cup milk

Preheat oven to 450 degrees.   20 servings

Cook the noodles for 1 minute and drain. Cream eggs with sugar. Add vanilla, noodles and butter. Combine sour cream, cheeses and milk. Add to noodle mixture. Pour into greased 9" x 13" baking pan. Bake at 450 degrees five minutes. Turn oven to 350 degrees and bake one hour.

PEACH HEALTH FOOD KUGEL (M)

```
1/2    lb. wide noodles, cooked and drained
3      eggs
1-1/2  cups cottage cheese
3/4    cup yogurt
8      ounces cream cheese
1/2    teaspoon vanilla extract
2      teaspoons cinnamon
1/4    cup honey
1/8    teaspoon salt
2      tablespoons melted butter
3      fresh ripe peaches, sliced
4      cups wide noodles, cooked and drained
```

Preheat oven to 375 degrees.   20 servings

Beat together everything except peaches and noodles. Now stir them in. Spread into greased 9" x 13" baking pan.

Topping:

```
3    tablespoons butter, melted
1    cup commercial bread crumbs, unseasoned
2    teaspoons cinnamon
1/4  cup wheat germ
1/4  cup brown sugar
some sliced canned peaches, in own juices, drained
a few maraschino cherries
```

Mix butter with bread crumbs, cinnamon, wheat germ and brown sugar. Spread on top of noodle mixture. Garnish with peaches and cherries after baking.   Bake 50 minutes.

94

✗ ✗ try

RASPBERRY YOGURT AND
APRICOT CHEESE KUGEL (M) ✡

1	lb. medium egg noodles
6	eggs, beaten
3	cups milk
1	cup sour cream
1	cup raspberry yogurt
1	pint cottage cheese
1/2	cup currants
1/2	cup apricot preserves
4	tablespoons sugar
1-1/2	teaspoon vanilla extract
6	tablespoons unsalted butter
1/4	cup confectioner's sugar
1/2	teaspoon cinnamon

Preheat oven to 350 degrees.   10 servings

Boil noodles three minutes and drain. Add eggs to
noodles and mix well. Combine milk, sour cream, yogurt,
cottage cheese, currants, preserves, sugar and vanilla;
stir well and add to noodles. Melt butter in 10" x 10"
baking pan and spread it around bottom and edges. Pour
mixture in and bake one hour. Invert into pan and
sprinkle with confectioner's sugar mixed with cinnamon.

FRUIT MEDLEY KUGEL (M)   *✗✗✗ yes*

1	lb. wide noodles, cooked and drained
4	eggs
1/2	cup sugar
1	small can crushed pineapple (drain, save juice)
6	ounces cream cheese
1	teaspoon vanilla extract
1	pint sour cream
1/2	cup maraschino cherries (halved)
1/2	cup raisins
1	apple, grated
6	pitted prunes, cut up

Topping for fruit medley kugel:

1/2	cup graham cracker crumbs
2	teaspoons sugar
3	dashes cinnamon

use Wert recipe but add cinnamon

Preheat oven to 350 degrees.   20 servings

Soften cream cheese in reserved pineapple juice. Mix
together well all ingredients. Pour into greased 9" x
13" pan. Mix together topping ingredients and sprinkle
over noodle mixture. Bake one hour.

ORANGE KUGEL (M)

1   lb. fine noodles
1   pint sour cream
1   lb. cream cheese
2   tablespoons cream cheese
1/4   lb. butter
10   eggs
2   cups sugar
3   cups whole milk
1   cup orange juice

Preheat oven to 350 degrees.   20 servings

In mixing bowl beat together sour cream, cream cheese
and butter. In a separate bowl beat together eggs,
sugar and vanilla. Beat together, in another bowl the
milk and orange juice. Combine everything. Pour into
greased 9" x 13" baking pan and bake 45 minutes.

ORANGE, PINEAPPLE AND CHERRY KUGEL (M)

8   ounces fine noodles, cooked al dente
8   ounces cream cheese
1/2   cup sour cream
1/2   cup sweet butter
1   cup sugar
1   teaspoon vanilla extract
4   medium eggs
1   large can mandarin oranges, drained
1   large can crushed pineapple, drained
1   large can dark sweet or
      Queen Ann pitted cherries, drained
cinnamon and sugar mixture

Preheat oven to 350 degrees.   20 servings

Blend all ingredients except fruit and noodles. Beat 10
minutes. Mix noodles and fruit with a spoon and stir
into cheese mixture. Pour into greased 9" x 13" pan.
Sprinkle with sugar and cinnamon. Bake one hour or
until set.

✗ try

FRUIT COCKTAIL DAIRY KUGEL I (M)

1   lb. medium noodles, cooked and drained
1/4 lb. margarine or butter
1   cup sugar
1   pint cottage cheese
1/2 pint sour cream
1   can fruit cocktail, 1 lb. size, drained *(sugarless)*
1   teaspoon vanilla
1/2 cup raisins
4   eggs, separated
a few slices of pineapple rings
some maraschino cherries

Preheat oven to 350 degrees.   20 servings

Melt butter and cream with sugar. Add cottage cheese,
sour cream, and vanilla. Separate eggs. Beat yolks and
add to butter, sugar, cheese mixture. Add noodles,
fruit cocktail and raisins. In separate bowl, beat egg
whites until stiff and gently fold into noodle mixture.
Pour into a greased 9" x 13" baking pan. Bake one hour.
Garnish with pineapple rings with cherries in the center
for a beautiful topping.

FRUIT COCKTAIL DAIRY KUGEL II (M) *try*

1   lb. medium noodles, parboiled and drained
3/4 cup sugar
1   cup milk
1/2 lb. whipped cream cheese
1   teaspoon vanilla extract
1/4 lb. plus 3 tablespoons butter or margarine
6   large eggs, beaten
2   tablespoons sour cream
1/2 cup raisins
1   1 lb. can fruit cocktail, drained *(sugarless)*

Preheat oven to 350 degrees.   20 servings

Cream sugar and margarine together. Add milk, cream
cheese, vanilla, eggs, and sour cream. Mix into
noodles. Add raisins and fruit cocktail. Pour into
greased 9" x 13" pan.

Topping:

1   cup corn flake crumbs
1/4 cup sugar mixed with 1 teaspoon cinnamon
5   tablespoons margarine or butter

Melt margarine and cream with sugar and cinnamon. Mix
into corn flakes. Sprinkle on top of noodle pudding.
Bake about 45 minutes or until firm.

KUGEL, KOOGLE, KIGLE (M)

```
12   ounces medium egg noodles, cooked and drained
5    eggs, beaten
1    small container cottage cheese
1    small container sour cream
6    ounces cream cheese
1/4  lb. butter
1    small can pineapple, drained
1/2  cup sugar
1    teaspoon vanilla extract
```

Optional: Add any of the following fruits --

> 1 small can mandarin oranges, drained
> 2 or 3 medium apples, peeled and sliced
> 1 small can peaches, drained
> 2 or 3 fresh peaches, peeled, sliced
> 1 cup mixed seedless grapes

> **Or spread on top --**

> pineapple, crushed
> cherries, prepared pie
> blueberries, prepared pie

> See "Make A Plain Kugel Fancy", p. 24

Preheat oven to 350 degrees.   20 servings

Mix in a large bowl all ingredients, not including
toppings. Pour into greased 9" x 13" pan. Bake without
toppings for about one hour. If toppings are used, bake
45 minutes. Add topping and bake an additional 15
minutes.

 ## CHERRY KUGEL (M)

```
1    lb. medium noodles, cooked and drained
6    eggs, beaten
1/2  cup sugar
1/2  cup milk
1/2  pint sour cream
16   ounces cream cheese, room temperature
1    pint creamed cottage cheese
1    teaspoon vanilla extract
1    can cherry pie filling
```

Preheat oven to 350 degrees.   20 servings

Melt cream cheese in warm milk. Add beaten eggs.
Combine with noodles and all other ingredients, except
cherries. Pour into greased 9"x 13" pan. Bake 40
minutes. Remove, cool, add fruit topping. Before
serving, return to oven 30 minutes. Serve warm.

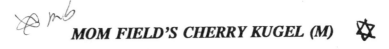

MOM FIELD'S CHERRY KUGEL (M) ✡

1/2 lb. fine noodles, cooked and drained
10 eggs, beaten
1   pint cottage cheese
3   ounces cream cheese
1   small can crushed pineapple, drained
1   cup sugar
1   teaspoon vanilla extract
1   jar cherry pie filling

Preheat oven to 350 degrees.   20 servings

Mash cottage cheese and cream cheese fine. Combine
everything except cherries. Pour into greased 9" x 13"
pan.   Bake 1/2 hour.   Add cherries and bake an
additional 1/2 hour.

POT CHEESE, APPLE AND CHERRY KUGEL (M)

1/2 lb. medium noodles, cooked and drained
1   lb. pot cheese or dry cottage cheese
1/2 lb. cream cheese
1/4 lb. butter
1   cup milk
1/2 cup sugar
1   teaspoon vanilla extract
5   eggs, beaten
2   apples, peeled and grated
1   jar prepared pie cherries
dabs of sour cream for topping

Preheat oven to 350 degrees.   20 servings

Mix together cheeses and butter. Add eggs, milk, sugar
and vanilla. Add noodles and apples. Pour into greased
9" x 13" pan. Bake one hour. Top with pie cherries and
serve with sour cream.

try ✕ mb

PINEAPPLE PRESERVES KUGEL (M)

1   lb. noodles, cooked and drained
1/2 lb. butter, melted
4   tablespoons sour cream
1/2 teaspoon cinnamon
1/3 cup sugar
1   jar pineapple preserves

Preheat oven to 350 degrees.   20 servings

Add all of the above ingredients to noodles. Pour into
9" x 13" pan. Prepare topping.

Topping For Pineapple Preserves Kugel:

2   tablespoons melted butter
1/2 cup chopped walnuts
1/2 cup corn flake crumbs
1/4 cup cinnamon and sugar

Combine above ingredients. Place topping over noodle
mixture. Bake one hour.

✕✕ try PINEAPPLE UPSIDE DOWN KUGEL (M)

1/2 lb. medium egg noodles, cooked and drained
1/3 cup butter
4   eggs
1/2 cup sugar
1   teaspoon grated lemon peel
1   tablespoon lemon juice
1/4 teaspoon salt
2   cups milk
1/2 cup firmly packed brown sugar
1   20 ounce can pineapple slices, drained
some maraschino cherries

Preheat oven to 350 degrees.   20 servings

Toss noodles with 3 tablespoons of the butter. Beat
together eggs, sugar, lemon peel and juice and salt;
stir in milk and add noodles. Melt remaining butter in
the bottom of a 9" square pan. Sprinkle brown sugar in
bottom of pan; arrange pineapple slices in pan and place
a cherry in center of each. Add noodle mixture. Bake
40 minutes or until set. Cool slightly. Invert onto
serving dish. Serve with whipped cream.

To sweeten a fresh pineapple, twist off the leafy top and place pineapple in microwave three minutes on high.

DAIRY DOUBLE PINEAPPLE KUGEL (M)

```
1/2 lb. broad noodles, parboiled and drained
3    eggs
4    tablespoons butter
1/2 lb. pot cheese or dry cottage cheese
8    ounces crushed pineapple with juice
1    cup sour cream
1    cup milk
1/2 cup sugar
1    teaspoon vanilla extract
1    teaspoon cinnamon
a few pineapple rings and maraschino cherries
```

Preheat oven to 350 degrees.   20 servings

Combine eggs and butter, pot cheese, sour cream and milk and beat well. Add sugar, crushed pineapple and juice, vanilla, and cinnamon. Mix well. Add noodles. Pour into greased 9" x 13" pan. Place pineapple rings on top, with a cherry in the middle of each ring. Bake 40-60 minutes, until golden.

DIET PINEAPPLE CHEESECAKE KUGEL (M)

```
1    cup thin noodles, cooked, drained
2    eggs
2/3  cups low fat cottage cheese
heat-stable sweetener equivalent to 6 teaspoons sugar
1/2 cup plain low fat yogurt
2    teaspoons vanilla extract
1    teaspoon vanilla butter-nut flavor
1/4 teaspoon ground cinnamon
1    cup pineapple, unsweetened, crushed drained
```

Preheat oven to 325 degrees. 8 servings 90 calories

In blender, combine eggs, cottage cheese, sweetener, yogurt, vanilla, vanilla butter-nut flavor and cinnamon. Blend until smooth. Pour into mixing bowl and add pineapple and noodles and stir thoroughly. Pour mixture into square baking dish sprayed with non-stick baking spray. Sprinkle with additional cinnamon. Bake 40 minutes until set.

PINA COLADA KUGEL (M)

1   lb. fine noodles, cooked and drained
6   eggs, beaten
1   pint sour cream
1   large can crushed pineapple, not drained
1   cup sugar
1/2 teaspoon vanilla
1   cup shredded coconut
cinnamon for sprinkling

Preheat oven to 350 degrees.   15 servings

Combine all ingredients. Pour into greased 9" x 13"
pan, sprinkle with cinnamon and bake for 1 hour.

BOSTON LUCKSHEN KUGEL (M)

1   lb. wide noodles, cooked and drained
1/2   lb. cream cheese
3/4   cup sugar
4   eggs
2   cups milk
1   small box instant banana pudding
1   teaspoon vanilla extract
2   tablespoons orange juice
1/2   pint sour cream
1-1/2 cups dried apricots

Topping:

2   cups corn flakes
1/2 stick margarine, melted
sugar and cinnamon, enough to sprinkle

Preheat oven to 350 degrees.   20 servings

Presoak apricots in water or brandy for 15 minutes.
Prepare banana pudding with the milk and set aside. In
a large bowl cream together cream cheese and sugar. Add
eggs, vanilla, orange juice and sour cream and mix
together. Add pudding, mixing thoroughly.   Add
noodles. Pour 1/2 mixture into a greased 9" x 13" pan.
Cover with apricots. Add the rest of the mixture. Top
with corn flakes, margarine, sugar and cinnamon. Bake
one hour. Top with cool whip for a heavenly dessert.

VIVIAN'S APRICOT KUGEL (M)

```
1   lb. medium noodles, cooked and drained
1/2 lb. margarine
1/2 lb. cream cheese
8   eggs, beaten
juice of one lemon
1   cup sugar
1/2 cup cinnamon and sugar mixture
3/4 lb. dried apricots
1   small jar maraschino cherries
```

Preheat oven to 350 degrees.   20 servings

Cook apricots in water until barely soft. Melt
margarine and cream cheese together. Add all
ingredients except apricots and cherries and mix.
Grease a 9" x 13" pan. Place a layer of apricots, cut
maraschino cherries and a sprinkling of cinnamon and
sugar. Then spread a layer of cheese and noodle
mixture. Repeat until finished. Top with cinnamon-
sugar mixture and cherries. Bake one hour.

CUSTARDY APRICOT KUGEL (M)

```
1/2 lb. fine noodles, cooked and drained
1/2 lb. cream cheese
1   small can apricot nectar ?
3   eggs, beaten
1/4 lb. margarine, melted
1   cup milk
```

Topping for Custardy Apricot Kugel:

```
1/2 cup sugar
2   cups crushed corn flakes
1/2 stick margarine, melted
1/4 cup brown sugar
```

Preheat oven to 350 degrees.   20 servings

Mix together noodles, cream cheese, nectar, sugar, eggs
margarine and milk. Pour into 9" x 13" pan sprayed with
non-stick baking spray. Prepare topping by mixing
ingredients together. Spread over noodle mixture. Bake
one hour.

APRICOT JAM KUGEL (M)

1/2 lb. wide noodles, cooked and drained

Mix the following ingredients together:

```
3    oz. cream cheese
3    eggs
1/2 cup sugar
3/4 cup apricot jam   ? sugarles
3/4 cup milk
3/4 stick margarine, melted
```

Preheat oven to 350 degrees.   20 servings

Beat the above ingredients well and add to noodles. Spread in greased 9" x 13" pan.

Top with:

```
1-1/2 cups crushed corn flakes mixed with:
1/4    cup sugar
1      teaspoon cinnamon
3/4    stick margarine, melted
```

Mix above ingredients and spread over noodle mixture. May be refrigerated at this point and baked the next day. Bake 45-60 minutes until browned and firm.

WONDERFUL KUGEL SOUFFLE (M)

```
8      ounces medium noodles, cooked and drained
1      cup sugar
8      ounces cream cheese, room temperature
1      teaspoon vanilla extract
8      eggs
1      pint sour cream
1-1/2 sticks margarine or butter room temperature
cinnamon and sugar, enough to sprinkle
```

Preheat oven to 350 degrees.   20 servings

Blend together the eggs, butter, cream cheese, sour cream, vanilla, and sugar. In greased 9" x 13" pan, line noodles on bottom. Pour mixture on top. Sprinkle with cinnamon and sugar mixture. Bake 45 minutes until puffy and browned like a souffle.

BLUEBERRY KUGEL (M)

Do everything the same as in "Wonderful Kugel Souffle" above, but do not sprinkle with cinnamon and sugar and use:

2 sticks butter instead of 1-1/2 sticks
2 teaspoons vanilla instead of 1 teaspoon
1 large can prepared blueberry pie filling.

use blueberry & splenda

Turn baked kugel out onto a serving platter. When it sets, the center will probably sink slightly, forming a well. Pour heated pie filling into the well. If center doesn't sink, spread the pie filling over entire top.

POT CHEESE, NUTS AND RAISINS KUGEL (M)

1/2 lb. fine noodles, cooked and drained
1 pint sour cream
1/2 lb. cream cheese, room temperature
1 lb. pot cheese or dry cottage cheese
4 eggs, beaten
1 cup sugar
1 teaspoon vanilla extract

Topping:

1/2 cup raisins
1 teaspoon cinnamon
1/2 cup chopped walnuts

Preheat oven to 350 degrees.   20 servings

Mix all ingredients except topping. Pour into greased 9" x 13" pan and bake 30 minutes. Remove and sprinkle with nuts, raisins and cinnamon. Bake 30 minutes more.

POT CHEESE AND WHITE RAISIN KUGEL (M)

1/2 lb. egg noodles, medium, cooked, drained
1 cup sugar
1 cup white raisins
1/2 lb. pot cheese or dry cottage cheese
1/4 lb. whipped cream cheese
1/4 lb. butter
3 eggs, beaten
2 cups milk
1/2 tablespoon vanilla flavoring

Preheat oven to 350 degrees.   20 servings

Stir butter into noodles until butter is melted. Add sugar, raisins, pot cheese, and cream cheese. Beat together milk, vanilla and eggs and add to noodle mixture. Bake in greased 9" x 13" baking pan 1 to 1-1/2 hours until set.

APPLE PIE FILLING AND ALMOND TOPPED KUGEL (M)

1/2 lb. medium noodles, cooked and drained
1/4 lb. butter or margarine
6   eggs, separated
1   cup sugar
1/2 lb. creamed cottage cheese
1/2 pint sour cream
4   ounces whipped cream cheese
1   teaspoon vanilla extract
1   jar prepared apple pie filling
some slivered almonds

Preheat oven to 350 degrees.   20 servings

Melt butter in 9" x 13" pan. Pour noodles into pan and stir in butter. Combine egg yolks with sugar, cottage cheese, sour cream, cream cheese and vanilla. Mix until smooth. Beat egg whites until stiff. Mix yolk mixture into noodles. Fold in egg whites. Bake 30 minutes. Remove and top with apples and almonds. Bake 15 minutes more.

DIANE'S APPLE KUGEL (M)

1   lb. medium noodles, cooked and drained
1/4   lb. butter or margarine
1-1/2 cups sugar
6   eggs, beaten
1/2   cup whole milk
dash cinnamon
dash salt
6   large apples, peeled and sliced

Preheat oven to 350 degrees.   20 servings

Add melted butter or margarine to cooked noodles. Add remaining ingredients and pour into greased 9" x 13" pan. Sprinkle liberally with cinnamon. Bake one hour, uncovered.

106

DIET APPLE KUGEL (M)

```
2/3      cup low fat cottage cheese
2        eggs
1        tablespoon margarine, melted
1/2      teaspoon ground cinnamon
2/3      cup nonfat dry milk
1-1/2 cups water
heat stable sweetener equivalent to 6 teaspoon sugar
2        teaspoons lemon juice
1-1/2 teaspoons vanilla extract
2        cups cooked thin or medium noodles
2        small, sweet apples,  peeled, coarsely chopped
```

Preheat oven to 350.   8 servings   140 calories each

In a blender, combine all ingredients, except noodles and apples. Blend until smooth. Pour into a bowl and stir in noodles and apples. Pour mixture into an 8" square baking dish that has been sprayed with non-stick baking spray. Sprinkle with additional cinnamon. Bake one hour, uncovered until set and lightly browned.

APPLE AND RAISIN NOODLE KUGEL (M)

```
1        lb. medium noodles, cooked and drained
3        eggs, beaten
3        tablespoons butter or margarine, melted
1-1/4 cups cottage cheese
1/2      cup sour cream
1/2      cup milk
1        cup apples, peeled, chopped
1-1/4 teaspoon lemon rind, grated
1/2      cup each sugar and raisins
1/2      teaspoon each cinnamon, nutmeg and salt
```

Preheat oven to 350 degrees.   8-10 servings

Combine all ingredients except nutmeg. Pour into greased 2-1/2 quart casserole. Sprinkle top with nutmeg. Bake 40-50 minutes. Serve hot as is or top with currant jelly for a scrumptious dessert.

handwritten: ⅟⅟ yes

STRAWBERRIES AND CREAM
PINEAPPLE KUGEL (M)

```
1/2  lb. of 1/2" wide noodles, cooked and drained
1    lb. creamed cottage cheese
1/2  cup sugar
2    eggs or 4 egg whites, well beaten
4    cups dairy sour cream
1    8 ounce can crushed pineapple, with juice
salt to taste (optional)
2    cups strawberries, fresh
```

Preheat oven to 350 degrees.   10 servings

Mash the cottage cheese until smooth. Blend the sugar,
eggs and 2 cups sour cream. Stir in cheese, noodles and
undrained crushed pineapple. Add salt if desired. Pour
into well-buttered 10" x 10" baking dish and bake
uncovered about one hour or until lightly browned. Serve
warm or cold topped with 2 cups slightly sweetened sour
cream and sweetened, sliced strawberries.

ABOUT HOW MY SISTER NANCY
MAKES KUGEL (M)

handwritten: Absolutely, Absolutely

*I have written this recipe exactly the way my sister, Nancy
Deutsch, gave it to me. She is a great cook and doesn't get too
hung up on "recipes." She is always ready to improvise.*

In a big bowl, mix with a spoon, not beater, 16 ounces
cottage cheese, 16 ounces sour cream, about 6 beaten
eggs, 1/2 cup (more or less) sugar, about 1/2 teaspoon
cinnamon, 1 teaspoon vanilla. Add plumped raisins, if
you like them....golden ones better than brown. Boil 8-
10 ounces thin noodles (about 3/8" wide) until al
dente....drain them. Mix the concoction together with
the noodles, put it in a greased up pan....bake about
30-40 minutes at 325-350 degrees, depending on how well
your oven works....Add crushed pineapple, cherries, or
blueberries, smeared on top, after about 20 minutes, if
you wish....Cool it off, serve with sour cream.

108

XXXX Absolutely Absolutely

LIKE-A-CINNAMON BUN KUGEL (M)

This kugel is oozing with scrumptiousness.

```
1/2    lb. medium noodles, cooked and drained
3      eggs, separated
1/2    pint sour cream
1/2    lb. cottage cheese
1/2    cup milk
1/2    cup sugar
1      small can crushed pineapple, drained
1/4    lb. butter
1/2    cup brown sugar
1/2    cup chopped walnuts
1/3    cup white raisins
1-1/2  teaspoons cinnamon
```

Preheat oven to 350 degrees.   10 servings

Add sour cream, cottage cheese, milk, sugar and pineapple to beaten egg yolks. Mix with noodles and fold in stiffly beaten egg whites. Melt butter in an 10" x 10" pan and spread evenly, coating bottom and sides. Sprinkle with brown sugar, cinnamon, walnuts and raisins and stir thoroughly. Now pour noodle mixture on top. Bake one hour. Invert onto serving dish when done. Garnish with more white raisins.

CUSTARD TOPPED KUGEL (M)

```
8      ounces fine noodles, cooked and drained
1/4 lb. margarine, melted
4      ounces cream cheese
8      eggs
1      pint sour cream
3/4 cup sugar
1      tablespoon vanilla flavoring
```

Topping:

```
2      cups crushed corn flakes
cinnamon and sugar mixture, enough to sprinkle
```

Preheat oven to 325 degrees.   20 servings

Pour margarine over noodles and stir. In separate bowl, blend together cream cheese, eggs, sour cream, sugar and vanilla. Pour noodle mixture into greased 10" x 10" baking pan. Then pour cream cheese mixture on top, DO NOT STIR. Top with corn flakes, cinnamon and sugar. Bake 45 minutes until firm and custardy.

CHEESE BLINTZES (M)

Blintzes are not kugel, however, the Blintzes Souffle is!

```
3/4 cup all purpose flour
1/2 teaspoon salt
1   teaspoon baking powder
2   tablespoons confectioner's sugar
2   eggs
1   cup milk
1/2 teaspoon vanilla extract
```

Sift together flour, salt, baking powder and confectioner's sugar. Beat together eggs, milk and vanilla extract. Make a well in center of flour and whisk in egg mixture. Let stand 1/2 hour at room temperature. Butter a 6" skillet or crepe pan. Drop 1/4 cup of batter into center of pan and gently move pan so batter spreads evenly and cook until edges turn light brown. Turn out onto a kitchen towel with brown side up. Butter pan again and repeat until all the batter is used.

Filling for blintzes:

```
1 lb. pot uncreamed cottage cheese
3-4 tablespoons sugar
dash cinnamon
1 egg
```

Mix all ingredients together. Spread browned side of crepe with filling in a log shape. Fold crepe up over filling and tuck in sides to cover. When all blintzes are filled and rolled, cook in pan with 3-4 tablespoons of melted butter until golden brown. Serve with sour cream and/or preserves.

 ## BLINTZES SOUFFLE (M)

```
12  mixed fruit or cheese blintzes, uncooked
1/4 lb. margarine or butter
1   teaspoon cinnamon
1   tablespoon vanilla flavoring
1/2 cup sugar
5   eggs
1   pint sour cream
```

Preheat oven to 350 degrees.   12 servings

Arrange blintzes in pan, one or two layers high. Have
all other ingredients at room temperature and mix them
together. Pour liquid mixture over blintzes. Bake 45
minutes or until top is set.

MAGNIFICENT KUGEL (M)

1	lb. medium noodles, cooked and drained
4	tablespoons pareve margarine, melted
1	cup cottage cheese
1	cup plain yogurt
4	tablespoons frozen orange juice concentrate
3	tablespoons light brown sugar
1/4	cup honey
5	large eggs, separated
1	teaspoon vanilla extract
1	tablespoon lemon juice
1	teaspoon grated lemon rind
1	pinch salt
1	teaspoon cinnamon
1/2	teaspoon nutmeg
2	apples, pared and coarsely chopped
1	cup soft pitted prunes
1	cup pitted dates, chopped
1	cup pineapple tidbits, drained
1/2	cup dark seedless raisins
1/2	cup nuts, chopped

Preheat oven to 350 degrees.   20 servings

Place orange juice concentrate and melted margarine in
a pot and heat until juice is dissolved. Pour over
noodles and toss. Beat together egg yolks, cottage
cheese, yogurt, vanilla extract, honey, lemon juice and
lemon rind. Add brown sugar, salt, cinnamon, nutmeg and
beat again. Add egg mixture to noodle mixture. Combine
apples, prunes, dates, pineapple tidbits, raisins and
nuts and toss. Add to noodle mixture and toss again
until fruits and nuts are evenly distributed. Fold in
stiffly beatem egg whites. Pour into large baking pan
that has been greased. Cover with foil and bake 30
minutes. Uncover and bake 15 or 20 minutes or until
set. Serve hot.

NOT SWEET DAIRY NOODLE KUGELS

Also see: Broccoli/Spinach Kugel, p. 128
Dairy Onion Noodle Kugel, p. 134
Mushroom and Sour Cream Kugel, p. 130
Viennese Noodle Pudding, p. 54

CHEDDAR CHEESE KUGEL (M)

This kugel tastes like macaroni and cheese, but better!

```
1    lb. medium egg noodles, cooked and drain
1/2  cup margarine, melted
4    eggs, beaten
2    cups sour cream
1    lb. cheddar cheese, grated
salt and pepper to taste
```

Preheat oven to 350 degrees.   20 servings

Grease pan with 2 tablespoons of the margarine, melted.
Combine everything else and pour into lightly greased
9"x 13" pan. Bake one hour.

NOT TOO SWEET CUSTARD KUGEL (M)

```
1    lb. noodles, cooked, drained
1/4  cup sugar
2    eggs, beaten
1/4  lb. butter
1    teaspoon vanilla extract
```

Topping:

```
1/2  lb. cottage cheese
1    cup sour cream
2    eggs
1/4  cup milk
1    teaspoon lemon juice
```

Preheat oven to 350 degrees.   20 servings

Combine noodles, eggs, vanilla, sugar and butter. Pour
into ungreased 9" x 13" pan. Mix topping ingredients in
blender. Pour over noodle mixture. Bake one hour.

EASY NOT SWEET DAIRY KUGEL (M)

try ms

1/2 lb. fine noodles, cooked and drained
1   pint cottage cheese
3/4 cup sour cream
4   eggs
2   tablespoons sugar
1   teaspoon salt
3   tablespoons melted butter
4   tablespoons dry bread crumbs

Preheat oven to 375 degrees.   10 servings

Beat eggs, sour cream, salt and sugar together. Add cheese and noodles. Pour into buttered 10" x 10" baking dish. Sprinkle with bread crumbs and butter. Bake 40 minutes.

NOT SWEET LAYERED NOODLE PUDDING (M)

try ms

1   lb. broad noodles, cooked and drained
1   lb. cottage cheese, drained
4   egg yolks
1/2 cup heavy cream
2   tablespoons sugar
1   teaspoon salt
1/4 cup bread crumbs
4   tablespoons melted butter

Preheat oven to 375 degrees.   20 servings

Cream cottage cheese in food processor or blender. Beat together cottage cheese, egg yolks, cream, sugar, and salt until smooth. In 9" x 13" pan sprayed with non-stick baking spray, arrange alternate layers of noodles and cheese mixture, starting and ending with noodles. Make as many layers as possible. Sprinkle with bread crumbs and butter. Bake 30 minutes.

 ## RICOTTA CHEESE KUGEL (M)

8   ounces wide noodles, cooked and drained
4   eggs, beaten
1/4 lb. butter
3   ounces cream cheese
1   pint sour cream
1   cup ricotta cheese
    juice of 1 lemon
3   tablespoons sugar
1   cup white raisins, plumped in hot water, drained

Topping:

1 cup corn flakes
4 tablespoons butter, melted

Preheat oven to 350 degrees.   10 servings

Mix together eggs. 1/4 lb. butter, sour cream, lemon
juice, cream cheese, ricotta cheese and sugar in food
processor. Pour into mixing bowl and fold in noodles
and raisins. Pour into greased 10" square baking dish.
Sprinkle corn flakes on top and drizzle with melted
butter. Bake one hour. Serve hot.

TANGY SOUR CREAM KUGEL (M)

8 ounces medium egg noodles, cooked and drained
1 tablespoon oil
2 tablespoons butter   3 eggs, separated
1 tablespoon sugar   1 pint sour cream
dash dry mustard   salt to taste

Preheat oven to 350 degrees.   8 servings
Put oil into 8" square pan and heat in preheated oven.
Add butter to noodles and mix thoroughly. Add sugar and
mix. Stir beaten egg yolks into noodles with dry
mustard. Add sour cream and salt, mix thoroughly. Beat
egg whites until stiff, and fold into noodle mixture.
Remove pan from oven. Pour in noodle mixture. Bake 1
to 1-1/2 hours until brown.

BUTTERMILK KUGEL (M)

12 ounces wide noodles, cooked and drained
4 eggs
1 quart buttermilk
1 lb. creamed cottage cheese
   salt and pepper
1 teaspoon sugar
2 tablespoons butter

Preheat oven to 400 degrees.   20 servings

Spread drained noodles evenly across the bottom of a
greased 9" x 13" pan. Beat together remaining
ingredients and pour over noodles. Dot with butter.
Bake one hour. Serve with sour cream and sweetened
frozen or fresh strawberries.

114

ye try

GREEN NOODLE KUGEL (M) ✡

8 ounces medium-wide spinach noodles or fettucini
1 cup uncreamed cottage or pot cheese
1 clove garlic, chopped
1 cup sour cream plus more for topping
1 onion, finely minced
salt to taste
dash of Tabasco sauce
1 tablespoon kosher Worcestershire sauce
Grated Parmesan cheese

Preheat oven to 350 degrees.   8 servings

Break noodles into 2-1/2 to 3 inch pieces and cook until
tender. Drain and combine with cottage or pot cheese,
garlic, sour cream, onion, salt, Tabasco, and
Worcestershire sauce. Butter a 1-1/2 quart casserole
and pour in mixture. Bake until brown and crusty on
top, about 45 minutes. Serve with Parmesan cheese for
sprinkling and additional sour cream.

NOT SWEET PAREVE NOODLE KUGELS

See the following recipes
in other chapters of this book:

Ashkenazic Salt and Pepper Kugel, p. 54

Diet Vegetable Noodle Kugel, p. 129

Onion Noodle Kugel, p. 135

Spinach Kugel with Orzo, p. 129

PAREVE NOODLE KUGELS

Pareve noodle kugels are Eastern and Central European (Ashkenazic) in origin. Some of the oldest recipes have been traced to the early Middle Ages in Germany.

To be kosher, pareve margarine or oil may used in pareve (P) recipes but never butter. If butter is used, the food must be considered to be milchig (M) or dairy.

SWEET PAREVE NOODLE KUGELS

Also see: Jerusalem Kugel, p. 67
Kugel, p. 52
Award Winning Kugel, p. 84

APPLES, RAISINS AND NUTS...

have been symbolic of sweetness and plenty. These ingredients are frequently used in kugels, especially for Rosh Hashanah, the Jewish New Year.

*** *Absolutely*
APPLE, RAISIN AND NUT KUGEL (P)

```
1    lb. wide noodles, cooked and drained
6    eggs, beaten
6    tablespoons pareve margarine, melted
Scant capful almond extract
1/2  teaspoon cinnamon
5-6  apples, peeled and cut into pieces
1/3  cup brown sugar
3/4  cup chopped walnuts
2    tablespoons lemon juice
1/2  cup raisins or currants
1/2  cup maraschino cherries
```

Preheat oven to 350 degrees.   20 servings

Combine all ingredients, except cherries. Mix well.
Pour into 9" x 13" baking pan sprayed with non-stick
baking spray. Garnish with cherries. Bake 50 minutes
or until set and golden brown.

ORANGE AND APPLE KUGEL

1   lb. noodles, fine, parboiled and drained
8   eggs, beaten
4   large apples, sliced and pared
1   cup raisins
Juice from 2 large oranges
2   tablespoons orange peel, grated
1   carrot, grated
1   teaspoon baking powder
1/4 teaspoon salt
1   cup brown sugar
1   teaspoon vanilla extract
1/2 cup oil

Preheat oven to 350 degrees.   24 servings

Mix everything together with noodles. Pour into greased
11" x 15" baking pan. Bake one hour.

APPLE AND PINEAPPLE KUGEL (P)

10   ounces wide noodles, cooked and drained
3   eggs, beaten
3/4 cups sugar
1   large can crushed pineapple, drained
5   apples cut in small chunks
1/4 cup oil
some maraschino cherries
cinnamon, enough for sprinkling

Preheat oven to 350 degrees.   20 servings

Combine noodles, eggs, sugar, drained pineapple, and
apples. Heat oil in 9" x 13" pan. Pour all mixed
ingredients into pan and decorate with maraschino
cherries. Sprinkle cinnamon on top. Bake one hour.
Freezes well. Best if baked day before serving and
refrigerated overnight.

APPLESAUCE AND JAM KUGEL (P)

3/4 lb. noodles, cooked 5-8 minutes and drained
1/2 stick pareve margarine
6   eggs, beaten
4   tablespoons brown sugar
1   pint applesauce

Topping:

1   cup corn flakes
1/2 cup jam (peach, apricot or prickly pear)

Preheat oven to 350 degrees.   20 servings

Add margarine to noodles and stir. Add beaten eggs, sugar and applesauce. Pour into greased 9" x 13" pan. Top with corn flakes. Bake 45 minutes. Spread with jam and return to oven for 1/2 hour.

Prickly pear jam, also known as cactus jam, is available in the Southwest and in specialty food stores throughout the United States. Native Israelis are called "Sabras" after this delicious fruit which is prickly and hard on the outside and sweet and soft on the inside.

STRAWBERRY, PINEAPPLE, APPLE KUGEL (P)

1/2 lb. medium noodles, cooked and drained
1   apple, peeled and grated
5   eggs, separated
1/2 cup strawberry preserves
8   ounces crushed pineapple, drained
2   tablespoons honey

Topping for Strawberry, Pineapple and Apple Kugel:

1/4 cup pareve margarine
cinnamon and sugar, enough for sprinkling
1/2 cup strawberry preserves

Preheat oven to 350 degrees.   10 servings

Combine beaten egg yolks, apple, 1/2 cup preserves, pineapple, and honey. Add noodles and thoroughly mix. Beat egg whites until stiff but not dry; fold into noodle mixture. Pour into 10" greased pan; dot top with margarine, cinnamon and sugar and dabs of the rest of the preserves. Bake 45 minutes, cool five minutes and serve.

PINEAPPLE NOODLE RING (P)

```
8    ounces medium egg noodles, cooked and drained
1/2  cup dark brown sugar
1    20 ounce can crushed pineapple, drained
4    eggs, lightly beaten
1    teaspoon vanilla extract
1    teaspoon cinnamon
1/4  cup pareve margarine, melted
```

Preheat oven to 350 degrees.   8-10 servings

Combine 2 tablespoons of brown sugar (from 1/2 cup) and 1/4 cup of crushed pineapple (from 20 ounce can) and spread mixture on bottom of an oiled ring mold (not a tube pan). Place noodles in a mixing bowl and add the remaining sugar, pineapple, eggs, vanilla, cinnamon and margarine, and combine thoroughly. Spoon the noodle mixture into mold and bake 50 minutes. Turn out onto a serving platter and serve hot.

CHERRY AND RAISIN KUGEL (P)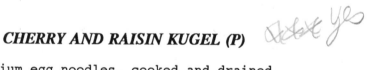

```
1    lb. medium egg noodles, cooked and drained
3/4  cup raisins
3/4  cup oil
10   maraschino cherries, cut up
3    tablespoons lemon juice
1    tablespoon lemon rind, grated
8    eggs, beaten
1    cup sugar
1    teaspoon vanilla extract
cinnamon, enough for spinkling
```

Preheat oven to 350 degrees.   20 servings

Combine everything except cinnamon. Stir well and pour into greased 9" x 13" pan. Sprinkle with cinnamon. Bake 45 minutes. Serve hot or cold.

120

PINEAPPLE, APPLESAUCE AND
RAISIN KUGEL (P)

```
1     lb. wide noodles, cooked and drained
3/4   cup sugar
1     small can crushed pineapple and juice
1     medium can apple sauce
2     cups apple juice
1/4   lb. parve margarine
1     cup non-dairy liquid creamer
1/2   cup raisins
1     tablespoon vanilla extract
5     eggs, beaten
```

Preheat oven to 350 degrees.   20 servings

Combine everything. Pour mixture into greased 9" x 13" pan. Sprinkle with cinnamon and sugar, if desired. Bake 45 minutes.

LEMON, PINEAPPLE KUGEL (P)

```
8     ounces wide noodles, cooked 12 minutes and drained
1     cup raisins
8     ounces crushed pineapple, drained
3     tablespoons lemon juice
4     eggs, beaten
1/2   cup each brown and white sugar
1     teaspoon salt
```

Preheat oven to 350 degrees.   8 servings

Combine noodles with above ingredients. Mix thoroughly. Pour into greased 8" baking pan.

Topping:

```
1 teaspoon cinnamon plus 1 tablespoon sugar
1 cup bread crumbs
2 tablespoons pareve margarine
1 teaspoon grated lemon rind plus 1 tablespoon lemon juice
```

Spread this mixture over noodle mixture. Bake 45 minutes until top is browned.

NADINE'S FRUITY KUGEL (P)

```
1    lb. wide noodles, cooked and drained
6    eggs, beaten
1    cup sugar
1    teaspoon vanilla extract
1/4  lb. pareve margarine
1    small can crushed pineapple, drained
1    large can fruit cocktail, drained
```

Preheat oven to 350 degrees.   20 servings

Cook noodles until done and drain. Mix with eggs, sugar, and vanilla. Grease 9" x 13" pan with 1 tablespoon margarine. Add remainder to mixture. Add fruit and mix well. Pour into pan. Bake one hour.

CONFECTIONERS' SUGAR KUGEL (P)

```
1/2  lb. fine noodles, cooked and drained
4    eggs, separated
1    cup confectioners' sugar
2    tablespoons grated almonds
     allspice
```

Preheat oven to 350 degrees.   8 servings

Beat egg yolks and sugar. Add almonds and noodles. Fold in stiffly beaten whites. Pour into greased 8" pan. Sprinkle with allspice. Set into pan filled one inch deep with water and bake 1/2 hour.

ASSORTED FRUIT KUGEL (P)

```
1    lb. broad noodles, cooked and drained
3    eggs, beaten
1    cup sugar
2    grated apples
1/3  cup orange juice
1    tablespoon orange rind, grated
3    tablespoons lemon juice
2    tablespoons lemon rind, grated
1/2  lb. pitted and cut prunes
1    cup small dried apricots
1/2  cup raisins
1/2  cup pareve margarine, melted
```

Topping for Assorted Fruit Kugel:

1/4 cup pareve margarine
1/4 cup matzah meal
1/4 cup brown sugar

Preheat oven to 350 degrees.   20 servings

Add all ingredients to cooked noodles. Pour into a greased 9" x 13" baking pan sprayed with non-stick baking spray. Sprinkle with topping. Bake one hour.

EASY APRICOT KUGEL (P)

1   lb. fine noodles, cooked and drained
1/4 lb. pareve margarine
6   eggs, beaten
1   jar apricot preserves

Preheat oven to 350 degrees.   20 servings

Combine all ingredients. Place in a greased 9" x 13" pan. Bake one hour.

 ## *DRIED FRUIT AND NUT MIX KUGEL (P)*

8   ounces medium noodles, cooked and drained
1/4 cup oil
1/4 cup sugar
1/4 cup pineapple or apricot jam *sugarless*
4   eggs
1   cup orange juice
1/2 teaspoon cinnamon
1/4 teaspoon ginger
      pinch salt
6   ounces mixed dried fruit and nut mix*
1   apple, with skin, diced

Preheat oven to 350 degrees.   10 servings

Toss noodles with 1/2 the oil. Beat together eggs, sugar and remaining oil. Add jam, orange juice, cinnamon, ginger and salt. Stir in dried fruit and apple. Add noodles and stir mixture thoroughly. Pour into greased 10" x 10" pan. Cover with foil and bake in preheated oven 40 minutes. Remove foil and bake 20 minutes more until firm and set. Serve warm or at room temperature.

* I like to use a trail mix that includes dried dates, papaya (great color) and pineapple, raisins, sunflower seeds, almonds and walnuts. Never use a mix that contains candy in a kugel.

FLUFFY PECAN NOODLE PUDDING (P)

8   ounces wide egg noodles, cooked 10 minutes, drained
4   eggs, separated
1/2 cup sugar
1/2 teaspoon cinnamon
1/4 cup pareve margarine, melted
1/2 cup seedless raisins
1/2 cup chopped pecans

Preheat oven to 350 degrees.   8 servings

Beat egg yolks, add sugar, cinnamon and butter. Beat
together until well blended. Combine with noodles and
add raisins and pecans. Beat egg whites until stiff and
fold into noodle mixture. Pour into 8" x 8" pan sprayed
with non-stick baking spray and bake one hour.

PRUNE JUICE KUGEL (P)

16 ounces wide noodles, cooked 15 minutes and drained
6   eggs, beaten
1/2 cup pareve margarine
1   cup brown sugar, well packed
1   cup raisins
2   teaspoons cinnamon

Topping:

sprinkling of cinnamon
1/2-1 cup bread crumbs, unseasoned
1/2 cup prune juice

Preheat oven to 350 degrees.   20 servings

Mix together everything except crumbs and juice. Pour
into greased 9" x 13" pan and brush top with prune
juice. Sprinkle with crumbs and cinnamon. Baste with
prune juice several times during baking. Bake 1 to
1-1/2 hour, until set.

APRICOT NOODLE PUDDING (P)

1   cup dried apricots
1/2 lb. broad noodles, cooked and drained
1   teaspoon salt
3   eggs, beaten
1/2 cup sugar
3   tablespoons graham cracker crumbs
1/4 teaspoon pareve margarine

124

Preheat oven to 350 degrees.   9 servings
Soak apricots in boiling water until soft. Beat eggs
and sugar until creamy and add to noodles. Drain soaked
apricots and sprinkle with graham cracker crumbs mixed
with cinnamon, saving a little for topping. Melt
margarine in square glass 9" baking dish and pour in
half of the noodle mixture. Spread apricots over this
and add remaining noodles. Sprinkle crumbs and cinnamon
mixture on top. Bake 40 minutes until browned.

APRICOT JAM KUGEL (P) ✡

1/2 lb. wide noodles, cooked and drained
3   teaspoons mayonnaise
3   eggs
1/2 cup sugar
3/4 cup apricot jam
3/4 cup pareve liquid creamer
3/4 stick pareve margarine, melted

Preheat oven to 350 degrees.   20 servings

Combine mayonnaise, eggs, sugar, jam, creamer and
margarine. Beat well and add to noodles. Spread in
greased 9" x 13" pan.

Topping:

1-1/2 cups crushed corn flakes   1   teaspoon cinnamon
3/4   stick margarine, melted   1/4 cup sugar

Mix above ingredients and spread over noodle mixture.
May be refrigerated at this point and baked the next
day. Bake 45-60 minutes until browned and firm.

GORGEOUS BUNDT PAN PECAN KUGEL (P) ✡

1/4 cup pareve margarine, melted
1/2 cup brown sugar
1/2 cup pecan halves
1/2 lb. broad noodles
2   eggs, beaten
1/4 cup pareve margarine, melted
1/2 teaspoon cinnamon
1/2 cup sugar
1/2 teaspoon salt

Preheat oven to 350 degrees.   8-10 servings
Melt 1/4 cup margarine and mix with brown sugar. Place
on bottom of a bundt pan. Arrange pecan halves with
pretty side down. Mix noodles with remaining ingredients. Pour into mold and bake 1 hour. Invert onto
serving platter.

·IV·
VEGETABLE KUGELS

&

ONION KUGELS

VEGETABLE KUGELS

Also see: Chicken Soup Matzah Kugel, p. 185
Diet Carrot Kugel, p. 183
Passover Carrot Kugel, p. 181

MOCK POTATO KUGEL (P OR M) ✡

Made with "flower" things

1   large cauli"flower"
1/3 cup wheat "flour" or 4 tablespoons potato starch
3   tablespoons saf"flower" oil
1   medium onion, peeled and cut into chunks
5   eggs, beaten
1/4 teaspoon white pepper
1/4 teaspoon nutmeg
Sun"flower" seeds to sprinkle over top

Preheat oven to 350 degrees.   9 servings

Combine cauliflower, onion, eggs, pepper and nutmeg in
a food processor. Using metal blade, process until
cauliflower is fine. Add wheat flour, oil and mix.
Pour into 9"-square baking pan sprayed with non-stick
baking spray. Top with seeds. Bake one hour until
golden brown. Serve topped with applesauce or for a
dairy kugel, melt Velveeta Cheese over top. Do not
freeze.

BROCCOLI/SPINACH KUGEL (M OR P) ✡

12 ounces medium noodles, cooked and drained
1 pint sour cream (or 3/4 pint pareve non-dairy
   creamer)
2 package pareve kosher onion soup mix
6 eggs
   dash pepper
2 sticks margarine cut into small pieces
2 packages chopped frozen spinach OR broccoli, cooked,
   drained and squeezed dry (don't mix vegetables, use
   2 packages of either)

<u>Optional Topping</u>:

1 cup corn flakes

Preheat oven to 375 degrees.   20 servings
Mix well all ingredients except vegetable and noodles.
Stir these in. Pour into greased 11" x 15" pan. Bake
about one hour until firm and browned.

SPINACH KUGEL WITH ORZO (M)

1 cup orzo pasta, cooked and drained
1 package chopped frozen spinach, cooked
4 large eggs
1/2 teaspoon Worcestershire sauce
1/4 teaspoon black pepper
1 cup ricotta cheese
1 cup fresh grated Parmesan cheese
1/3 cup dry bread crumbs

Preheat oven to 350 degrees.   8 servings

Pour cooked spinach into a colander and press with paper towels to remove excess moisture. Beat together 3 eggs, Worcestershire sauce, salt and pepper and add cheeses, spinach and orzo. Grease a 9" square baking pan and evenly sprinkle with bread crumbs. Pour mixture into pan. Beat remaining egg and brush on top of mixture. Bake for 40-45 minutes.

CABBAGE KUGEL (P)

8 ounces medium noodles, cooked and drained
1 cup onion, diced
2 cups cabbage, shredded
3 tablespoons oil
3 large eggs, beaten
1/2 teaspoon salt
1/4 teaspoon freshly ground pepper

Preheat oven to 350 degrees.   6-8 servings

Saute onions and cabbage in oil. Add eggs, salt, pepper and noodles. Pour into 8" greased baking pan and cover with foil. Bake for 20 minutes and uncover. Bake for an additional 25 minutes.

DIET VEGETABLE NOODLE KUGEL (P)

1 lb. medium noodles, cooked and drained
2 cups yellow onions, chopped
3 cups carrots, grated
2 cups mixed green and red bell peppers, chopped
2 tablespoons oil
5 large eggs, beaten
1 teaspoon black pepper, course or fresh ground
1 teaspoon salt or to taste

Preheat oven to 350 degrees. 20 servings 120 calories

In large pan, saute onions and peppers in 2 tablespoons
oil. Toss in carrots -- if not enough moisture, add
about 2 tablespoons of water. Do not overcook
vegetables. You just want them a little bit soft. Add
salt and pepper, then eggs and noodles. Pour into 9" x
13" baking pan sprayed with non-stick baking spray.
Bake 45 minutes to one hour or until browned nicely on
top.

MUSHROOM AND SOUR CREAM NOODLE KUGEL (M)

8   ounces medium egg noodles, parboiled and drained
4   tablespoons oil
1   large onion, chopped
8   ounces fresh mushrooms, diced
     salt and freshly ground pepper to taste
3/4 teaspoon paprika
2   large eggs, beaten
1   cup sour cream
3   tablespoons chopped fresh parsley

Preheat oven to 350 degrees.   10 servings

Saute onion in oil until tender. Add salt, pepper, 1/4
teaspoon paprika and mushrooms and saute until onions
are browned. Add more oil if necessary. Combine eggs,
sour cream and parsley and onion mixture and noodles.
Pour into greased 10" x 10" pan. Sprinkle with
remaining 1/2 teaspoon of paprika. Bake 30 minutes.
Serve topped with sour cream.

DIET SPAGHETTI SQUASH KUGEL (M)

2   cups spaghetti squash (save the shell)
1   egg
1/2 cup part-skim ricotta cheese
4   tablespoons raisins
1   package heat-stable artificial sweetener
1   tablespoon powdered sugar
1/2 teaspoon cinnamon

Preheat oven to 350 degrees. 4 servings   75 calories

Beat egg and add ricotta cheese, raisins, sweetener,
sugar and cinnamon. Fold in cooked squash. Pour into
empty squash shell. Place on cookie sheet. Bake 20
minutes.

BEATIFUL ZUCCHINI KUGEL (P)

```
3       zucchini, pared
2       bunches broccoli, stalks only
2       carrots
1       potato
1       large onion, peeled
3       eggs
1/3     oil
1-1/2   teaspoons salt
dash    freshly ground black pepper
```

Preheat oven to 350 degrees.   9 servings

Grate zucchini, broccoli stalks, carrots, potato and onion. Beat together eggs, oil, salt, and pepper and combine with vegetables. Pour into 9-inch baking pan sprayed with non-stick baking spray. Bake 1-1/2 hours until solid and golden. Do not freeze.

UGLY ZUCCHINI KUGEL (P)

```
1     lb. zucchini (2 medium)
2     teaspoons sugar
1/4   teaspoon salt
1     teaspoon cinnamon
1/2   cup raisins
1/4   cup chopped walnuts
3     tablespoons cooking oil or pareve margarine
1     small onion, chopped fine, sauteed
4     eggs, beaten lightly
```

Preheat oven to 350 degrees.   8 servings

Pare, grate and drain zucchini. Add sugar, salt cinnamon, raisins, and walnuts. Saute onion in oil until golden and add to zucchini mixture with eggs. Pour into greased 8" x 8" baking dish. Bake 40 minutes until lightly browned. Do not freeze.

ONE CUP VEGETABLE KUGEL (P)

1   cup carrots, grated and pared
1   cup sweet potatoes, grated and pared
1   cup white potatoes, grated and pared
1   tart apple, grated and pared
1   cup raisins
1   cup brown sugar
1   cup flour
1   teaspoon baking soda
1/4 teaspoon cinnamon
1/2 teaspoon salt
3/4 cup pareve margarine
1   teaspoon nutmeg

Preheat oven to 325 degrees.   10 servings

Spray a 10" casserole or muffin tins with non-stick
baking spray. Mix all ingredients together well. Pour
into baking dish. Cover with aluminum foil and bake 45
minutes in preheated oven. If using muffin tins, bake
30 minutes. Raise oven to 350 degrees, remove foil, and
bake 15 more minutes. Do not freeze.

ONIONS

Onions have been popular in Jewish cooking for thousands of years. They grew almost everywhere in the Diaspora, were easy to preserve and were used in many ways -- as seasoning and eaten alone as a vegetable. Yemenites ate them for dessert, candied.

Onions have been scientifically proven to be good for the heart, especially if eaten in conjunction with garlic. However, they do have a negative effect on some peoples' digestive systems (not to mention their breath). Therefore, I suggest that one should eat them in moderation.

Tzibble (onion) Kugels have been around probably for as long as there have been kugels. Actually, I had never heard of Tzibble Kugel until I started collecting recipes for this book. When I mentioned it to Mom Yellin, she was ecstatic. She loves it but never had prepared one and had not eaten Tzibble Kugel in many, many years. So, good daughter that I am, I made one for her! She was a very happy mom.

ONION KUGELS

Also see: Onion Chopping Hints, p. 21
          Kasha and Onion Kugel, p. 155
          Potato Kugels, p. 140
          Vegetable Kugels, p. 128

TZIBBLE KUGEL (P)

```
5   eggs, separated
1/2 cup oil
pinch salt and pepper
1/2 cup matzah meal
2   cups onions, finely chopped
```

Preheat oven to 350 degrees.   8 servings

Beat egg yolks. Add onion, oil, matzah meal, salt and pepper. Mix well. Beat whites to form stiff peaks and fold into mixture. Pour into greased 8" square pan. Bake 30 minutes.

DAIRY ONION NOODLE KUGEL (M)

```
1   lb. wide noodles, cooked and drained
1/4 lb. butter, melted
8   ounces whipped cream cheese
1   pint sour cream
1   large white onion, chopped
4   eggs, beaten
salt and pepper to taste
```

Preheat oven to 350 degrees.   10 servings

Combine everything. Pour into greased 10" baking pan. Sprinkle with bread crumbs, paprika and dot with butter. Bake one hour.

MUSHROOM AND ONION KUGEL (F)

```
8 ounces wide noodles, parboiled and drained
4 large onions, diced
5 tablespoons oil
2 eggs, beaten
2 tablespoons flour
salt and pepper to taste
1 cup mushrooms, diced  paprika
1 cup kosher chicken bouillon
```

Preheat oven to 350 degrees.   10 servings

Brown mushrooms and onions in oil. Add flour, then slowly stir in bouillon. Stir until thick. Add to noodles. Season to taste with salt and pepper. Pour into greased 10" pan. Pour eggs over top and sprinkle with paprika. Bake 30 minutes. Top with additional browned mushrooms and onions if desired and serve.

ONION BARLEY KUGEL (F)

1 cup pearl barley
4 cups kosher consomme, chicken or beef
2 teaspoons salt
1/2 lb. chopped mushrooms
2 onions, diced
2 tablespoons oil or chicken fat
1/4 teaspoon pepper
2 eggs, beaten

Preheat oven to 350 degrees.   8 servings

Boil consomme and stir in salt and barley. Cook for 10 minutes over medium heat, stirring occasionally. Cover and cook 45 minutes or until soft. Drain any excess water. Brown onions and mushrooms in fat and add to barley. Add pepper and eggs. Pour into greased 8" pan. Bake 40 minutes or until browned and set.

ONION NOODLE KUGEL (P OR F)

1 lb. fine noodles, cooked and drained
1 cup diced onions
1 cup oil or chicken fat
6 eggs, beaten

Preheat oven to 375 degrees.   10 servings

Brown onions in oil. Set aside to cool. Add eggs to noodles. Add browned onions and oil. Turn into a greased 10" square pan. Bake 40 minutes or until browned.

STOVE TOP ONION AND CHICKEN LIVER KUGEL (F)

1 lb. medium noodles, cooked and drained
8 eggs, beaten
1 medium onion
1/2 lb. chicken livers
1/2 cup oil
1 teaspoon fresh dill
dash of salt, pepper and garlic powder

Saute onions in oil and broil chicken livers. Sprinkle with salt, pepper, garlic powder and dill. Mash or dice chicken livers. Add eggs and noodles. Cook stove-top; see instructions for stove-top cooking, p. 22.

Note: *Some cuts of meat must be broiled to abide by laws of Kashruth. Liver is one of those meats.*

ONION-RAISIN KUGEL (P)

1   lb. medium noodles, cooked and drained
1/2 cup white raisins, chopped
1/2 cup onions, chopped
4   tablespoons pareve margarine
3   eggs, beaten

Preheat oven to 375 degrees.   8 servings

Soak raisins in cold water for 15 minutes. Brown onions in margarine and allow to cool. Add eggs, noodles, and raisins. Pour into greased 8" square pan and bake for 40 minutes.

SWEET ONION KUGEL (P)

1   lb. medium noodles, cooked and drained
2   large onions
1/4 teaspoon salt
1/4 teaspoon pepper
3   eggs, beaten
1/2 cup bread crumbs
2   tablespoons apricot preserves
1/2 cup brown sugar
2   tablespoons pareve margarine

Preheat oven to 350 degrees.   15 servings

Grease 9" x 13" baking pan and place in oven while oven is preheating, about 10 minutes. Brown onions and combine them with noodles, eggs, 2 teaspoons brown sugar, breadcrumbs, salt and pepper. Pour mixture into warmed pan. Sprinkle with remaining brown sugar and dot with butter and apricot preserves. Bake for 40 minutes until browned and crispy.

136

·V·

HANUKKAH
LATKES
&
POTATO KUGEL

HANUKKAH

About 2,100 years ago, under the leadership of Judah Maccabee, the Maccabean army was victorious over the Syrians. Legend tells, when the people of Judea were about to light the menorah to rededicate the Temple, only one small cruse of oil was found -- enough for just one day. A miracle happened and the oil lasted eight days, long enough for new holy olive-oil to be pressed.

That is why Jews celebrate Hanukkah, the Festival of Lights. The word Hanukkah means dedication. The holiday has been celebrated since 165 B.C.E. on Kislev 25 on the Jewish calendar. It lasts for eight days and a menorah called a Hanukkiah is used. A new candle is added each day from right to left and is lit by a "servant" candle called a "shammas" from left to right until all eight are aglow. After lighting the candles while chanting a prayer, songs are sung and presents are opened. Games are played with a four-sided top called a dreidel.

Eating food that has been prepared in oil during Hanukkah is a tradition for Jews in many parts of the world. It is a reminder of the miracle that happened when the Temple in Jerusalem was rededicated. In Spain and Morocco a rolled donut that has a sugar glaze called Fichuelas de Hanukkah is eaten. In Israel a raised jelly donut called Sufganiyot is served at Hanukkah time.

Since the Middle Ages, Middle Eastern Sephardic Jews have traditionally eaten cheese latkes. It is said that this custom evolved from the story of Judith. To say Holofernes did not treat her well is an understatement. She stuffed him with cheese so that he would become thirsty. He drank wine to quench his thirst and when he was asleep in a drunken stupor, she----I can't go on. What happened is too horrible to tell. However, the story of Judith was thought to have been an inspiration to the Maccabees. So people started baking cheese-filled things for Hanukkah. From the cheese latkes, cheese kugels were derived.

The largest proportion of American Jews are Ashkenazic (Eastern European) and it is their tradition that has become the most popular in this country. Because potatoes are inexpensive, easy to grow and very filling, they became a staple food of the Ashkenazic Jews. Potato latkes (pancakes) made with grated potatoes, eggs, and onions and fried in goose fat became a popular item and a traditional Hanukkah food. The same batter was poured into pottery crocks or baking tins and was baked in a slow oven overnight for the Sabbath. This became known as "potato kugel."

On the Sabbath of Hanukkah an old Eastern European Jewish tradition was to bake two kugels -- one in consideration of the Sabbath and the other to help glorify Hanukkah.

POTATO KUGEL

Pop Yellin came from a large and poor family (nine kids). His dad died when Pop was 12 years old. They ate a lot of potatoes because they were so inexpensive. His mother prepared them in every possible way. On the Sabbath she prepared them Pop's favorite way, in a kugel.

Pop Field also came from a large, poor family (eight kids). When his mom made potato kugel, she made it crisp and browned on the outside with a thick crust. It was soft and wonderful on the inside. She made her kugel in a heavy iron skillet on top of the stove.

The beverage for the evening was a glass of "2 cents plain." When my father was a very young boy, he would be sent to the corner soda shop with a beautiful pitcher that is now sitting in my china cabinet. The kindly soda man would fill it for 2 cents with what we know today as "seltzer." When Dad got a little older, the squirt bottles came into existence. I remember the squirt bottles from my childhood. My Aunt Myrna told me they are still around in Florida and New York.

POTATO KUGEL

Also see: Mock Potato Kugel, p. 128
           One Cup Vegetable Kugel, p. 132

✗✗✗ Absolutely

FAVORITE POTATO KUGEL (P) ✡

*This batter can also be used to make potato pancakes

12   medium white potatoes, with skin, grated, well drained
2   large onions, without skin
2   large carrots, brushed, grated
1/4 cup matzah meal

1   tablespoon salt
1/2 teaspoon white pepper
4   eggs, beaten
1/4 cup oil

Preheat oven to 375 degrees.   20 servings

Grate potatoes and vegetables in food processor. Add remaining ingredients and mix thoroughly. Pour into oiled 9" x 13" baking pan*. Bake one hour or until top is browned and crisp at edges. Do not freeze.

If you want to have the same "feeling" as eating the fried latkes, but don't want the fat, pour the batter into individual muffin tins sprayed with a non-stick baking spray and bake 1/2 hour at 350 degrees until firm. Serve with applesauce and (if for a dairy meal) sour cream. Also good served with sugar to sprinkle on top instead of applesauce or sour cream.

Note: To prevent potatoes from turning black, place pared potatoes in a bowl of water with some lemon juice added.

For lighter kugel, separate eggs. Add beaten yolks and 2 teaspoons baking powder. Fold stiffly beaten whites into potato mixture.

STOVE TOP POTATO KUGEL (P)

4   potatoes, unpeeled, grated and well drained
1/4 cup pareve margarine
1   large onion, chopped
2   eggs, beaten
2/3 cup matzah meal
1   teaspoon salt

Saute onions until tender in margarine. Remove with
slotted spoon and combine with potatoes, eggs, matzah
meal and salt. Pour into skillet and press down. Cover
and cook on low flame until bottom is well browned.
Flip over and brown other side with cover removed.

MILK POTATO KUGEL (M)

6   medium white potatoes, with skin, grated, well
     drained
1   large onion, peeled and chopped
2   eggs, beaten
1   cup milk
1/2 teaspoon salt
1/4 teaspoon pepper
3   tablespoons oil

Preheat oven to 325 degrees.   6 servings

Mix potatoes together with salt, pepper, eggs and milk.
Brown onion in oil until soft and add, with oil, to
potato mixture. Pour into greased 8" pan and bake 1-1/2
hours until browned. Do not freeze.

MASHED POTATO KUGEL (P)

4 cups potatoes, cooked, drained and mashed
salt and pepper to taste
4 eggs, beaten
2 tablespoons grits
4 tablespoons pareve margarine
1 teaspoon onion powder

Preheat oven to 375 degrees.   8 servings

Combine all ingredients and mix well. Pour mixture into
a well greased baking pan and bake 45 minutes or until
browned.

LAYERED FISH AND POTATO KUGEL (M)

5	medium white potatoes, thinly sliced
3	cups fish, cooked or canned, flaked
4	tablespoons butter
2	onions, sliced
1/2	teaspoons pepper
1-1/2	teaspoons salt

1-1/2 cups light cream
2 eggs

Preheat oven to 350 degrees.   8 servings

Melt butter in skillet and brown onions in it. Arrange alternate layers of potatoes, fish and onions in buttered 8" baking dish, starting and ending with potatoes. Sprinkle potatoes with salt and pepper. Beat eggs and cream together and pour over the contents of baking dish. Bake 45 minutes until lightly browned. Do not freeze.

Variation:

Use smoked salmon (lox) instead of other fish. Eliminate salt and use 1 cup light cream and 1/2 cup milk.

DIET POTATO KUGEL (P)

6	medium white potatoes, with skin, grated, drained
6	eggs, separated
2	medium onion, peeled and grated
6	tablespoons all-purpose flour
3	tablespoons oil
2-1/2	teaspoons light salt
3/4	teaspoon white pepper
2-1/2	teaspoons baking powder

Preheat oven to 375.   10 servings   170 calories

Combine potatoes, egg yolks, onion, flour, oil salt, pepper, and baking powder. Mix well. Beat egg whites in another bowl until stiff. Thoroughly fold them into the potato mixture. Spoon into baking pan sprayed with non-stick baking spray. Bake one hour until set and lightly browned.

CREAM CHEESE AND POTATO KUGEL (M)

4   medium all purpose potatoes, grated
1/4 cup onion, chopped
18 ounces cream cheese, softened
3   eggs, beaten
1/4 cup margarine, melted
1/4 cup flour, presifted, unbleached
1/2 teaspoon baking powder
1/2 teaspoon salt

Preheat oven to 350 degrees.   6-8 servings

Blend together cream cheese, eggs and margarine. Add flour, baking powder and salt. Stir in potatoes and onions. Pour into greased 8" x 8" baking pan and bake for 50 minutes.

HANUKKAH SABBATH MENU

SOUP

Cabbage Borscht

ENTREE

Roast chicken
Bread Stuffing Kugel
Potato Kugel
Steamed whole green beans and sliced mushrooms

DESSERT

Rice Kugel served with non-dairy whipped topping

AMERICAN HANUKKAH PARTY

Mini Potato Kugels made in muffin pans and/or
Latkes -- a variety or just potato
Applesauce and/or Sugar for topping

Sliced meats including:
Turkey, Roast Beef, Corned Beef, Pastrami

Real (imitations will not do) hard crusted, sliced
Jewish Rye, Pumpernickel and Rolls

Cole slaw
Pickles and olives
Sliced assorted vegetables
Mayonnaise, Russian dressing, catsup, mustard

Mandel Broit, Strudel and Chocolate Hanukkah Gelt

CABBAGE BORSCHT (F)

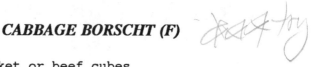

2-1/2 lbs. brisket or beef cubes
2   quarts boiling water
2   lbs. cabbage
1   large onion
salt to taste
1/2   cup lemon juice
4   tablespoons brown sugar
1   large can stewed tomatoes
1   cup dried lima beans or 1 can, drained

Soak lima beans overnight in water or cheat and use drained canned limas. Cut brisket into chunks; cover with water and bring to boil. Turn heat to simmer and, with a spoon, skim the "scum" that will form on top of water. Cut onion and cabbage into chunks and add to broth. Add lemon juice, salt, brown sugar, lima beans and stewed tomatoes. Cover pot and cook two hours or until lima beans and meat are tender. Serves 6.

STEAMED WHOLE GREEN BEANS
AND MUSHROOMS (P)

1   lb. package frozen whole green beans or 1 lb. fresh
1/2 pound of mushrooms, sliced
1   small onion, chopped
1   tablespoon oil
lemon juice, to taste

If fresh green beans are used, wash them and cut off the ends. Saute mushrooms and onion in oil until tender. Place green beans into a saucepan with 1/2 cup water. Steam about four minutes or until slightly tender but still crispy (or not frozen anymore). DO NOT OVERCOOK to retain nutritional value. Add sauteed mushrooms and onions. Sprinkle with lemon juice.

LATKES

It would be fun to have a Hanukkah party with a variety of latkes such as potato, vegetable, fruit and cheese. In my family, however, we always just had the potato kind and served them with the other wonderful foods in the "American Hanukkah Party Menu" on p. 145.

Uncle Sam Yellin from Stratford-Laurel Springs, N. J. made the best potato latkes. He used to serve them with leg of lamb smothered in thick brown gravy. My husband, Steve, picked up where Uncle Sam left off with the potato latkes. However, Steve never got the knack of how to make the lamb quite the same and neither did I.

My friend Zina Gorelik is from Belorus or Belorussia. She told me potato latkes originated there and she prepared a wonderful luncheon meal for me with latkes stuffed with ground meat. In Belorus Jewish people were not familiar with kashruth and latkes prepared in this manner are frequently topped with sour cream. The ground beef is usually mixed with ground pork but for me Zina mixed it with ground turkey.

STUFFED POTATO LATKES

1/4 lb. mixed ground beef and ground turkey
1   small onion
1/2 teaspoon each dried dill, parsley, and caraway seeds
1   egg
pinch of salt and pepper
Steve's Potato Latke recipe but use 3 tablespoons of flour

Thoroughly combine everything except latke batter. Heat oil in a large frying pan. With a large spoon, place latke batter into a pan. Cover with ground beef and top with more batter. Cover pan with a lid and fry until golden on one side. Flip latkes to other side. Fry until golden and remove from pan and serve. Makes 8 patties.

Variation: Boil 1/2 lb. mushrooms, drain and slice. Saute mushrooms in a little oil with 1 small chopped onion. Use to stuff latkes instead of ground meat.

STEVE'S POTATO LATKES (P)

This recipe can also be used to make potato kugel

```
6     medium white potatoes, grated and drained
2     eggs
1     teaspoon salt
1/4   teaspoon black pepper
1     large onion
1     heaping tablespoon flour
enough oil for frying
```

Grate potatoes*. Stir in the rest of the ingredients. Pour 1/2 inch oil into fry pan. When bubbles form after small drops of water are added to oil, it is ready. Drop batter into hot oil with a large spoon and flatten. Fry until golden brown around edges and turn with spatula. Fry flipped side until golden brown. Remove from pan and place on paper towels. Add more oil if necessary and repeat until all of the batter is used. Pancakes are best when served right after cooking. When reheated they lose crispness. Serve with applesauce or sugar for sprinkling. For a wonderful dairy dish serve with sour cream.

Note: Best pancakes are about 4" in diameter. Too large cook unevenly, too small get too crisp.

* Steve is very particular about how his potatoes are grated. They must be done by hand on the medium holes of the grater. He also must use his favorite large wooden spoon when placing the batter into the hot oil.

If you use a food processor to grate potatoes and you only have one size hole for grating -- if finer shred is desired, return course shreds to processor and use steel blade as you pulse process to desired consistency.

WHITE AND SWEET POTATO LATKES (P)

1   cup sweet potatoes, grated
1   cup white potatoes, grated
1   medium onion, grated
1/4 cup matzah meal
2   eggs
1-1/2 teaspoons salt
dash of pepper
enough oil for frying

Combine everything. Pour 1/2 inch oil into fry pan. When bubbles form after small drops of water are added to oil, it is ready. Drop batter into hot oil with a large spoon and flatten. Fry until golden brown around edges and turn with spatula. Fry flipped side until golden brown. Remove from pan and place on paper towels. Add more oil if necessary and repeat until all of the batter is used. Pancakes are best when served right after cooking. When reheated they lose crispness. Serve warm.

NO-FRY POTATO LATKES (P)

3 cups mashed potatoes
1 large egg, beaten
salt and pepper to taste

Preheat oven to 350 degrees.

Mix potatoes and egg together and form into patties. Place on greased cookie sheet and bake 30-45 minutes or until browned.

CHEESE LATKES (M)

2   cups dry cottage cheese
1   cup sifted flour
1/2 teaspoon salt
2   eggs
2   tablespoons sugar
enough oil for frying

Separate eggs. Beat egg yolks with sugar and salt. Add cottage cheese and flour. Beat egg whites until stiff and fold into mixture. Oil a large frying pan or griddle. Drop batter onto hot pan by the tablespoonful and flatten with spoon. Cook until golden brown around edges and turn with spatula. Cook flipped side until golden brown. Add more oil if necessary and repeat until all of the batter is used. Serve plain or sprinkled with sugar and cinnamon or preserves.

FRUIT LATKES (P)

```
2       cups flour
1/2     teaspoon salt
3       teaspoons baking powder
2       eggs, beaten
1-1/3   cups orange juice
1       small can crushed pineapple, drained
confectioners' sugar for sprinkling
```

Sift together flour, salt and baking powder and beat in egg and orange juice. Add crushed pineapple. Oil a large frying pan or griddle. Drop batter onto hot pan by the tablespoonful and flatten with spoon. Cook until golden brown around edges and turn with spatula. Cook flipped side until golden brown. Add more oil if necessary and repeat until all of the batter is used. Sprinkle with powdered sugar. Serve warm. Best served right after cooking. When reheated they lose crispness.

VEGETABLE LATKES (P)

```
1 cup mushrooms, sliced
1 cup zucchini, shredded
1 cup carrots, shredded
1 tablespoon garlic, chopped
salt and fresh ground pepper, to taste
1 large egg, beaten
3 tablespoons flour, unbleached, presifted
```

Combine vegetables and spices. Add egg and stir, then add flour and stir until everything is thoroughly mixed. Heat about 1/4 cup of oil in large frying pan. When bubbles form after small drops of water are added to oil, it is ready. Drop batter into oil by the tablespoonful. Fry until golden brown around edges and turn with spatula. Fry flipped side until golden brown. Remove from pan and drain on paper towels. Add more oil if necessary and repeat until all of the batter is used. Repeat process until all batter is used. Serve warm. Best served right after cooking. When reheated they lose crispness.

CORN LATKES
OTHERWISE KNOWN AS FRITTERS (P or M)

```
2    cups cooked corn
2    eggs, beaten
1/2 teaspoon salt
1/2 cup flour
1/2 cup water or milk
```

To the eggs add salt, flour and liquid to make a smooth batter. Add corn and stir thoroughly. Oil a large frying pan or griddle. Drop batter onto hot pan by the tablespoonful and flatten with spoon. Cook until golden brown around edges and turn with spatula. Cook flipped side until golden brown. Add more oil if necessary and repeat until all of the batter is used. Serve warm. Best served right after cooking. When reheated they lose crispness.

·VI·
GRAIN
PASTRY & BREAD
kugels

GRAIN KUGELS

Also see: **Bulgur and Nut Kugel, p. 68**
Middle Eastern Farina Kugel, p. 66
Pyota Greek Style Farina Kugel, p. 65

MILLET KUGEL (P)

```
3     cups water
1     cup millet grains
2     cups diced celery
2     cups grated apple, with skin
2     eggs, beaten
1     cup raisins
1/2   cup sunflower seeds
1/2   teaspoon cinnamon
2     teaspoons grated orange rind
1/2   teaspoon light salt
1/2   teaspoon vanilla
```

Preheat oven to 350 degrees.   10 servings

In a large skillet, bring water to a boil. Add millet gradually while stirring. Cook on low for 30 minutes or until all the water is absorbed. Stir remaining ingredients into cooked millet. Pour into 10" baking pan sprayed with non-stick baking spray. Sprinkle lightly with cinnamon. Bake about 30 minutes. *Serve for breakfast topped with your favorite yogurt -- I like strawberry-banana low-fat.

Yogurt topping makes this a dairy kugel.

Millet can be purchased at most health food stores and can sometimes be found in bulk food sections in supermarkets.

CORNMEAL KUGEL (M)

```
1        cup cornmeal
1        cup flour, presifted, all-purpose
1        teaspoon baking powder
1/2      teaspoon salt
1/2      cup creamed cottage cheese
1-1/2    cups plain yogurt
1-1/2    cups sour cream
5        tablespoons butter or margarine, softened
3/4      cup sugar
3        large eggs, separated
```

Preheat oven to 350 degrees.   8 servings

Combine dry (first four) ingredients. In a separate
bowl combine cottage cheese, sour cream and yogurt. In
another separate bowl cream butter with 1/2 cup sugar.
Add egg yolks and beat until smooth. Stir in cheese
mixture alternately with dry ingredients. In ANOTHER
separate bowl, whip whites until they form soft peaks.
Add remaining 1/4 cup sugar and beat until whites are
stiff and shiny but not dry. Fold whites gently into
cheese mixture. Pour into greased 8" x 8" baking pan.
Bake 45 minutes or until center comes out dry. Serve
warm with sour cream.

KASHA AND ONION KUGEL (P)

```
1    lb. medium noodles, cooked and drained
1    cup kasha (groats), cooked
4    onions, chopped
1    clove garlic, minced
1/3  cup each margarine and oil
1/4  lb. fresh mushrooms, sliced
1/2  teaspoon each salt and pepper
4    eggs, beaten
```

Preheat oven to 350 degrees.   15 servings

Combine kasha, noodles and add eggs. Saute onions,
mushrooms and garlic in hot oil and margarine and add
salt and pepper. Add onion mixture to kasha mixture and
mix well. Pour into greased 9" x 13" pan and bake for
45 minutes.

RICE KUGELS

Absolutely

CREAMY RICE KUGEL (M)

1	cup white rice, cooked
5	eggs, beaten
2-1/2	cups whole milk
1	can evaporated milk
8	ounces whipped cream cheese
1/4	lb. butter or margarine, softened
1/4	cup sugar
1	cup white raisins
1	tablespoon vanilla
2-1/2	teaspoons cinnamon

Preheat oven to 350 degrees.   8 servings

Combine rice, eggs, milks, cream cheese, butter or margarine and sugar. Add raisins, vanilla and cinnamon and mix well. Pour into greased 9" x 9" pan. Bake for 1-1/4 hours until top is golden. Serve cold.

PINEAPPLE RICE KUGEL (P)

2	cups cooked white rice
2	teaspoons sugar
1/2	cup brown sugar
1	large can crushed pineapple, NOT drained
1/2	stick margarine
2	eggs

Preheat oven to 350 degrees.   8 servings

Mix cooked rice with undrained pineapple. Blend in beaten eggs, melted butter and sugar. Pour mixture into greased 8" casserole and bake 45 minutes.

PINEAPPLE RAISIN AND
NUT RICE KUGEL (P)

3   cups rice, white or brown, not instant, cooked
1/2 cup white sugar
1/2 cup brown sugar
1/4 cup oil
1   teaspoon grated lemon peel
1   teaspoon cinnamon
1/2 teaspoon vanilla extract
3   eggs
1/2 cup raisins
1/2 cup crushed pineapple with juice
1/2 cup walnuts, chopped

Preheat oven to 350 degrees.   8 servings

Beat together sugar, oil, lemon peel, cinnamon and vanilla. Add eggs, one at a time, then rice, combining thoroughly. Stir in raisins, pineapple and walnuts. Pour into greased 8" square pan. Bake one hour or until golden. Excellent served warm or cold.

Serving suggestion: For a delicious cold dessert, top with whipped cream. However, this recipe will then become a dairy dessert.

ORANGE RICE KUGEL (M)

3   cups rice, white or brown, not instant, cooked
1   cup light cream
1   cup orange juice
1/4 cup orange liqueur
4   eggs, beaten
1/2 cup sugar
1   teaspoon grated orange rind
1/4 teaspoon allspice
1   small can mandarin oranges, drained
2   tablespoons flour, unbleached, presifted
3/4 cup raisins
1/2 teaspoon salt

Preheat oven to 375 degrees.   10 servings

Mix everything together. Pour into greased 10" square pan and bake one hour. Serve warm topped with whipped cream for dessert.

PAULA'S RICE PUDDING (M)

NO! This is not a kugel but it's great for parties!

```
1-1/2 cups rice, uncooked
1/4   lb. butter
2     eggs, slightly beaten
3     cups milk
1-1/2 cups sugar
1     large can evaporated milk
1     cup raisins (optional)
```

Cook rice according to package directions. Add all of
the ingredients and cook to boiling.   Add 1 tablespoon
vanilla and 1 tablespoon cinnamon. Continue to cook 2-3
more minutes. Soak raisins in hot water until plump and
drain. Add to rice pudding. Pudding will be thin, but
will thicken as it cools.

PASTRY KUGELS

Also see: Rumanian Kugel Balls, p. 58
              Steamed Pear Kugel, p. 60

*The next three recipes seem to be similar, but each has a look
and taste that is uniquely its own. The textures are similar to
some of the old-fashioned steamed kugels.*

MERBERTEIGE PASTRY APPLE KUGEL (P)

```
1     Merberteige Pastry (see recipe)
8     cups thinly sliced apples
3/4   cup fine bread crumbs
1-1/4 cups sugar or honey
1     teaspoon cinnamon
1/2   teaspoon nutmeg
6     tablespoons oil
```

Preheat oven to 400 degrees.   10 servings

Combine everything except pastry. Prepare Merberteige
Pastry.

158

MERBERTEIGE PASTRY (P)

1/3   cup pareve margarine
1-1/3 cups flour, unbleached, presifted
1-1/2 tablespoons brown sugar
pinch of salt
1   jumbo or 2 small egg yolks
3   tablespoons ice water

Cream butter or margarine. Add dry ingredients and work with two knives until particles are like sand. Add beaten yolk to water and lightly stir into dry ingredients. Knead into a ball. Divide pastry dough into three balls and roll to 1/4 inch thickness. Place one pastry on bottom of deep dish pie pan or casserole dish and spread with 1/3 apple mixture. Repeat twice, drizzle top with oil. Cover with foil and bake 45-50 minutes. Remove cover and bake 10 minutes longer until lightly browned on top.

LAYERED STRUDEL DOUGH KUGEL (P)

Dough:

3   cups flour, unbleached, presifted
1-1/2 tablespoons oil
2   eggs
3/4   cup lukewarm water (approximately)
1/4   teaspoon salt

Sift flour and form a well. Combine beaten eggs with oil, salt and water. Stir mixture into the center of flour, working in with a pastry cutter or two knives until it forms a ball of dough. Place on floured pastry board and knead until smooth and elastic. Warm mixing bowl and turn over dough to cover. Let stand at least 30 minutes before rolling, thin as possible. Brush surface of dough with oil and stretch, placing hands underneath and working from the center toward the outer edges until stretched evenly and paper thin.

Filling:

4   cups apples, thin sliced and pared
3/4 cup oil
1/2 cup sugar
2   teaspoons grated lemon rind
4   tablespoons lemon juice
1   teaspoon cinnamon
1   cup chopped walnuts
2   cups raisins
4   tablespoons flour
1/2 cup pareve dry bread crumbs

Preheat oven to 375 degrees.   10 servings

Combine all ingredients, except oil. Divide dough into
four equal parts. Place one stretched layer in
casserole or deep pie pan. Brush with oil. Spread 1/3
of mixture and repeat process two more times. End with
dough and brush with oil. Let stand 10 minutes, then
bake one hour until nicely browned.

GIANT STRUDEL KUGEL (P)

*The crust on this kugel tastes like my Bubby's wonderful strudel,
but the shape is much different from the little log pastries she
once made.*

Dough:

1-1/4 cups flour, unbleached, presifted
1/2   teaspoon baking powder   4 tablespoons warm
1   egg   water
1/4   teaspoon salt   2 tablespoons oil
1   tablespoon sugar

Sift dry ingredients together. Add oil and egg, and
water to bind. Turn out onto a floured board. Knead
until smooth and spongy. Set in bowl, sprinkle with
flour, cover with plastic wrap and chill 30 minutes.

Filling:

3   lb. baking apples, pared and sliced
1/2 cup raisins
1   teaspoons lemon juice
1/4 cup sugar
1   teaspoon cinnamon
1/4 teaspoon allspice
1   teaspoon vanilla extract

Preheat oven to 350 degrees.   15 servings

Combine ingredients in a bowl. Roll dough very thin, to
length of cookie sheet. Place dough on greased cookie
sheet (half will be hanging over edge). Brush with oil.
Spread apple mixture along long end. Fold remaining
dough over apples and pinch together edges. Brush top
with beaten egg. Bake 50 minutes until browned. Lift
off pan with <u>three</u> spatulas (you'll need another hand).

BUBBY'S STRUDEL

My Bubby used to make the best strudel. It was not like the apple strudel that is usually sold in the delis or bakeries. Hers was embellished with nuts, coconut, jam and raisins. I haven't tasted any bakery strudel like hers.

Dough:

2-1/2	cups flour, unbleached, presifted
1	teaspoon baking powder
1/2	teaspoon salt
2	tablespoons sugar
4	tablespoons oil
2	eggs
8	tablespoons warm water

Sift dry ingredients together. Add oil and egg, and water to bind. Turn out onto a floured board. Knead until smooth and spongy. Set in bowl, sprinkle with flour, cover with plastic wrap, and chill 30 minutes. Divide dough into five balls. Roll each ball very thin. Brush dough with oil.

Filling:

1	box white raisins
1	lb. nuts, chopped
2	teaspoons cinnamon
4	tablespoons sugar or
1	cup sweetened shredded coconut and omit sugar
10	ounces apricot, pineapple or raspberry jam

oil for brushing
Preheat oven to 400 degrees. Makes about 40 pieces

Rinse raisins in colander under hot water. Mix together with the rest of the filling ingredients. Divide into five portions. Spread one portion over one brushed and rolled-out piece of dough. Roll up like a jelly roll. Repeat until all dough is used. Put rolls in well-oiled baking pan. Turn to coat. Cut 1-1/2 inch slices 3/4 way through rolls. Bake 40-50 minutes until browned.

✗ ✗ ✗ Absolutely

KNISHES (P)

QUESTION: *If strudel dough kugel can be called kugel,*
can knishes ever be called kugel?

ANSWER: *No! Knishes are always knishes.*

Dough:

3   cups flour, unbleached, presifted
1   teaspoon salt
1/2 lb. pareve margarine
7   tablespoons ice water

Makes enough dough for 48 cocktail size knishes.

Combine salt and flour and add margarine. Blend with a
pastry cutter until mixture is like course meal. Add
ice water and knead with your hands to form into a ball.
Add a little more water if dough is too crumbly. Divide
in half. Lightly flour each ball of dough and wrap in
plastic. Refrigerate one hour or overnight.

POTATO FILLING FOR KNISHES (P)

6   medium all purpose potatoes, peeled
3   tablespoons pareve margarine
3   tablespoons oil
2   large onions, chopped
1/2 teaspoon salt
1/2 teaspoon fresh ground pepper
2   eggs, beaten

Cook and drain potatoes. Mash with potato masher until
smooth and add margarine. Saute onions in oil until
golden but still slightly crisp. Add onions, salt,
pepper and eggs to potatoes. Follow instructions given
on next page to complete knish preparation.

SWEET CHEESE FILLING FOR KNISHES (M)

```
1-1/2  lb. dry pot cheese
2      eggs, beaten
1/4    cup sugar
1/4    cup dry bread crumbs
1      tablespoon orange juice
```

Combine all ingredients. Follow instructions given below to complete knish preparation.

KASHA FILLING (P)

```
1/2  cup kasha (buckwheat groats or kernels)
1    cup boiling water
2    large eggs, beaten
4    tablespoons oil
1    medium onion, chopped
4    ounces mushrooms, chopped
salt and pepper, to taste
```

Heat skillet and add 2 tablespoons of oil. Add eggs and kasha and stir about three minutes, keeping grains separated. Add boiling water and cook about 15 minutes until all water is absorbed. Pour the other 2 tablespoons of oil into another skillet and saute mushrooms and onions until onions start to brown on edges. Sprinkle with salt and pepper. Combine mushrooms and onions to prepared kasha and allow to cool. Follow instructions given below to complete knish preparation.

TO COMPLETE KNISH PREPARATION

Preheat oven to 350 degrees.

Roll out dough on lightly floured board to about 1/8" thickness. Cut dough with a glass. Place 1 to 2 teaspoons of filling mixture in center of circle. Fold edges up over filling. Moisten dough at the top with a little water, if necessary, to make it stick together. Beat one more egg and brush over knish tops. Bake 20 minutes, until golden brown.

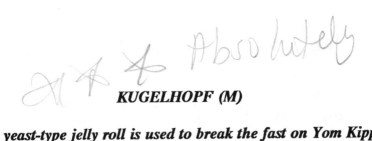

KUGELHOPF (M)

This yeast-type jelly roll is used to break the fast on Yom Kippur (the day of Atonement) in Hungary. It is definitely not a "kugel", however, its ingredients are very similar and I love the name!!!

4-1/2 packs active dry yeast
6   cups sifted flour   1-1/4 cups butter
2-1/2 cups sugar   3   eggs
2   cups lukewarm milk   1   teaspoon salt

Combine yeast, 2 tablespoons flour, 1 teaspoon sugar and milk. Cover with towel and set in a warm place to rise. Cream butter and remaining sugar. Add egg yolks and continue mixing until batter is thick and yellow. Put remaining flour into a large bowl. Make a hole in the center and put the yeast mixture into it, with egg mixture. Sprinkle salt and beat dough with spoon until it comes loose from sides and bottom of bowl. Cover again with a cloth and set aside in warm place to rise until doubled, about one hour.

Set aside:
1 egg and vanilla powdered sugar*
* place powdered sugar in a jar with a vanilla bean and cover tightly. Let stand overnight.

Filling:
2   tablespoons melted butter
3-1/2 tablespoons sugar
1/2   cups white raisins
1   tablespoon cinnamon
1   teaspoons each vanilla, orange and lemon extract

Preheat oven to 350 degrees.   10 servings

Mix together filling ingredients. When dough has risen, place it on a floured board and knead well with your hands. Roll it out, spread the filling mixture over it and roll it up, around the filling like a jelly roll. Brush with beaten egg and sprinkle with vanilla sugar. Bake one hour.

BREAD KUGELS

Also see: Fruit and Spice Kugel, p. 163
Kugel, p. 52
This Needs Some Gravy Kugel, p. 58

The world's most popular dessert kugel-type food is bread pudding. It most resembles a kugel when it is prepared with more bread than custard. Bread pudding is an internationally popular food and because of its many varieties, it is in a class of its own. However, it can be considered a kugel if all of the ingredients used in its preparation are kosher and if its consistency is firm like a bread. Any type of stale bread is fine*. Challah is especially good.

* White bread is sometimes not kosher since lard is frequently used as a shortening.

BREAD PUDDING (M)

4   cups stale bread cubes
2   cups milk
4   tablespoons butter
2/3 cup sugar
1/2 cup raisins
2   eggs
1/8 teaspoon salt
1/2 teaspoon grated nutmeg
1   teaspoon vanilla extract

Preheat oven to 350 degrees.   6 servings

Scald milk and add butter and sugar. Stir until butter has melted and sugar has dissolved. Pour over the bread and raisins and let stand for 20-30 minutes. Add salt, nutmeg and vanilla to well beaten eggs. Add to bread mixture. Pour into a greased 1-1/2 quart pan. Bake one hour, until firm. Serve topped with whipped cream or heavy cream.

Poultry stuffing, filling or dressing (however, you say it), when baked outside the bird in a baking pan, casserole dish or prepared stove-top (see HINTS section of this book) can also be called kugel. You save about 600 calories by baking stuffing in this manner.

Absolutely

MOM YELLIN'S BREAD STUFFING KUGEL (P or F)

```
1    large green bell pepper, diced
1    medium to large onion, diced
2    stalks celery, without leaves, diced*
1/4 lb. pareve margarine or 1 cup chicken broth
1    small loaf good bread** with crust, torn into pieces
4-6 eggs, or 8-12 egg whites
garlic powder, salt, pepper, paprika to taste
```

Preheat oven to 350 degrees.   8 servings

Saute green pepper, onion, and celery in margarine or chicken broth. Sprinkle generously with garlic powder, salt, pepper, and paprika. Break bread into large mixing bowl. Add vegetables with margarine or broth and enough eggs or egg whites to moisten thoroughly. Knead with your hands, checking to make sure the mixture is thoroughly moistened. Pour into greased casserole pan. Bake about one hour until firm and browned or cook stove-top (see instructions in "Hints" section of book).

* **Variation:**

Use 2 cups shredded carrots and 1 cup of sliced mushrooms instead of celery.

** **Use only pareve breads in pareve or fleishig recipes that call for bread. White bread is usually not pareve and is sometimes not kosher since lard is frequently used as a shortening. Challah (twisted egg bread) is a favorite.**

FRUIT AND NUT BREAD KUGEL (P) ✡

```
8    slices challah, cubed
1/2  cup pareve margarine
1    cup sugar
4    eggs, beaten
20   ounce can crushed pineapple, drained
1/3  cup walnuts, chopped
1    apple, peeled and thinly sliced
2    tablespoons wheat germ
cinnamon for sprinkling
```

Preheat oven to 350 degrees.

Cream together eggs, sugar and margarine. Add bread, apples, nuts and pineapple. Pour into greased 10" square pan. Sprinkle with wheat germ and cinnamon. Bake for 1 hour or until brown.

· VII ·

passover

kugels

PASSOVER

The first night of the eight-day holiday of Passover is celebrated on the night of the spring full moon -- the 15th of Nisan, the first spring month on the Jewish calendar. It is a double celebration: the Feast of Unleavened Bread and the springtime Festival of Freedom.

Most people in the world celebrate the arrival of spring. It is the season when new crops grow and there is hope of a good harvest. On this holiday God is thanked for things that grow and for new birth. It is believed by scholars that long before the Jews went into Egypt, while they were still shepherds, the first Jews celebrated the coming of spring. When Jews settled in Canaan they became farmers, and spring became even more important.

A terrible famine hit Canaan and since there was nothing to eat, except in Egypt, the Jews relocated. The Israelites lived in peace with their neighbors for several generations but were eventually enslaved. God became angry and sent 10 plagues. The last plague came on the night of the old spring festival of the lamb sacrifice. That plague was the death of the first-born. Jews marked their doorposts with the blood of sacrifice from a lamb, so the Angel of Death would "pass over" their houses.

Under the leadership of Moses, the Israelites were redeemed from slavery. After the Angel of Death passed, the Jews quickly left Egypt. They had to leave so fast that there was no time for the dough for the next day's bread to rise. It was prepared without leavening and baked and this wafer-like unleavened bread became known as matzah. Matzah is served throughout the holiday and is used in a large variety of ways in kugel recipes.

Every year Passover reminds the Jewish people that no

person is truly free as long as another is enslaved, in fear, hungry, or the victim of prejudice. Jews celebrate their freedom from winter and once again go outside and plant and grow things. They rejoice over nature and at the same time celebrate their history.

Before the holiday begins in Ashkenazic homes, the kitchen is thoroughly cleaned so that not one speck of "chametz" remains. Chametz includes bread, cereals, pasta and rice and all grain products except matzah and its derivatives.

Pots, pans, dishes and utensils used throughout the year are put away and those used only during Passover are brought out of storage. Foods containing products that are not kosher for Passover are given away so there is nothing left in the house that is not Pesahdic (for Passover).

Passover (*Pesach* in Hebrew) is celebrated with a religious service, known as a seder, around the dinner table. During the seder (which means order) a small book known as a Haggadah is read. It is read in Hebrew and is also translated so that everyone will understand what it tells. It includes history, explanations, stories, prayers, and songs. The male head of the family usually leads the seder and everyone in attendance participates in some way.

During the seder symbolic foods are referred to and some are tasted. They include horseradish as a reminder of the bitterness of slavery; a roasted lamb shank or roasted chicken neck as a reminder of the sacrifices at the Temple; a hard boiled egg to symbolize the continuance of life; salt water for bitter tears; celery or parsley to celebrate spring; haroset, a mixture of apples, nuts and cinnamon as a reminder of bricks the slaves were forced to make in Egypt.

After the seder, dinner is served. The appetizer, soup, main course and dessert are usually traditional foods. The meal would be basically the same as the Sabbath Friday Night and Holiday Meal (see menu) but food served must be approved for Passover. Roast lamb is frequently served during this holiday by Sephardic Jews. Ashkenazim most often will serve chicken and only root vegetables are allowed.

KUGELS PREPARED WITH MATZAH

are very popular during this holiday

Ingredients used in all Passover kugels must be approved "Kosher for Passover." Be sure to check labels on dairy products.

1. Only use kosher for Passover oil, margarine and jams.

2. In pareve Passover recipes, use pareve and kosher for Passover margarine.

3. Extracts are not kosher for Passover.

4. Confectioners' sugar is not OK for Passover since it contains corn starch.

5. Baking soda is a pure product and not a leavening agent and can be used for Passover.

6. Use canned fruits that are packed in their own juices.

SWEET PASSOVER KUGELS

DAIRY MATZAH KUGEL (M)

```
4    cups matzah farfel, soaked and drained
5    eggs, separated
1/4  cup sugar
1    cup milk
1    lb. cottage cheese
3    tablespoons melted butter
1    teaspoon salt
2    teaspoons cinnamon
1/2  cup raisins (optional)
```

Preheat oven to 350 degrees.   20 servings

Mix together everything except egg whites. Beat egg
whites until stiff. Fold into matzah mixture. Pour
into greased 9" x 13" pan. Bake 40 minutes. Serve warm
with sour cream for topping.

ORANGE DAIRY KUGEL (M)

```
5    matzahs
2    cups sour cream
2    cups dry cottage cheese
3    eggs
1/4  cup sugar
juice of one orange
1    tablespoon orange rind
```

Preheat oven to 350 degrees.   8 servings

Wet matzahs under running water. Mix together remaining
ingredients. In a greased 8" square pan. Layer matzah
and sour cream mixture, ending with sour cream mixture.
Bake 40 minutes.

BANANA YOGURT KUGEL (M)

6   matzahs, broken, soaked and squeezed
4   eggs
2/3 cups sugar
1   cup banana yogurt
1   cup dairy sour cream
1/2 cup crushed pineapple in own juice, drained
1   teaspoon cinnamon
1   cup mashed ripe bananas or fresh strawberries

Topping:

1 tablespoon sugar
1 teaspoon cinnamon
2 tablespoons Passover margarine
1 small jar apricot or pineapple preserves, melted

Preheat oven to 350 degrees.   8 servings

Combine matzahs, eggs, sugar, yogurt, sour cream, pineapple, vanilla, cinnamon, and bananas or strawberries. Pour into a greased 8" square baking pan. Combine sugar and cinnamon and sprinkle over kugel; dot with margarine. Bake 45 minutes until center is firm. Heat preserves to melt and then brush over kugel. Serve warm.

PASSOVER NOODLE FRUIT KUGEL (P)

1   box Passover noodles, cooked and drained
2   apples, pared and sliced
1   20 ounce can crushed pineapple in own juice, drained
1/4 lb. Passover margarine, melted
4   eggs
3/4 cup sugar
1   cup dried apricots, diced

Preheat oven to 375 degrees.   9 servings

Mix everything together. Pour into greased 9" x 9" pan. Bake 50 minutes.

Note: Noodles made from derivatives of matzah can be found in some grocery stores during Passover.

174

MATZAH KUGEL WITH APPLES AND NUTS (P) ✡

```
6    matzahs (egg or plain)
6    eggs, separated
1/2  cup raisins (optional)
6    tart apples, sliced thinly and peeled
1    cup chopped walnuts or slivered almonds
1    cup sugar or honey
1/2  teaspoon cinnamon
1/3  cup orange juice
1/3  cup lemon juice
1    tablespoon grated lemon rind
1/2  cup pareve Passover margarine, melted
```

Preheat oven to 350 degrees.   15 servings

Soak matzah and drain. Beat egg yolks, sugar, and cinnamon. Stir in juices, rind, matzahs, raisins, apples, walnuts and melted butter. Beat egg whites until stiff and fold into mixture. Sprinkle with cinnamon and sugar. Bake in greased 9" x 13" pan 45 minutes.

STEAMED THREE-BOWL APPLE PASSOVER KUGEL (P)

First Bowl - Combine in a small size bowl:

2/3 cup brown sugar plus a little extra to sprinkle
4   teaspoons oil

Second Bowl - Combine in a large size bowl:

5 matzahs, broken, soaked and drained
2 apples, peeled and grated
2 teaspoons cinnamon
3 teaspoons sugar
1 teaspoon lemon rind, grated
2 eggs, beaten

Third Bowl - Combine in a medium size bowl:

4   apples, peeled and sliced
2   tablespoons lemon juice
1   cup raisins
4   tablespoons your favorite Passover jam *sugarless*
1/4 cup sugar

Assemble Steamed Three-Bowl Apple Passover Kugel:

Preheat oven to 325 degrees.   9 servings

Grease a 9" x 9" pan. Sprinkle with a little brown
sugar and then spread with first mixture. Top with half
of second mixture, then spread on third mixture. End
with balance of second mixture. Set in the center of a
roasting pan and surround with water or a cholent. Bake
1-1/4 hours. Serve hot as a side dish or as dessert.

PEACH, APPLE AND RAISIN FARFEL KUGEL (P)

Tastes like a cobbler.

1/2 cup matzah farfel, soaked and drained
1/2 cup matzah meal
1/4 cup sugar
1   medium can sliced peaches, drained
1/2 stick pareve Passover margarine, melted
2   eggs, beaten
3   apples, sliced
1/2 cup raisins
cinnamon and sugar for topping

Preheat oven to 350 degrees.   8 servings

Mix together all ingredients except cinnamon and sugar.
Pour into 8" x 8" pan sprayed with non-stick baking
spray. Sprinkle with cinnamon and sugar mixture and
bake 45 minutes. Serve with poultry as a sweet side
dish or for dessert topped with ice cream for a dairy
dessert.

MATZAH MEAL KUGEL (P)

3/4 cup matzah meal
6   eggs, separated
1/4 cup cold water
1/2 teaspoon salt
1/4 teaspoon pepper
1/4 cup Passover oil
1/4 cup sugar

Preheat oven to 350 degrees.   8 servings

Beat yolks with water. Add everything except whites.
Beat whites until stiff, not dry and fold into mixture.
Pour into greased 8" x 8" pan and bake 1/2 hour.

176

MATZAH KUGEL WITH
PRUNES AND APRICOTS (P)

```
6    matzahs
12   ounces prunes, pitted
6    ounces dried apricots
3    cups water
2    teaspoons salt
2    medium apples, grated
6    eggs, beaten
1/4  cup sugar
```

Preheat oven to 350 degrees.   20 servings

Cook prunes and apricots five minutes in water and drain, but save 2 cups of the water. Soak matzahs in the water where fruits were cooked. Add all the remaining ingredients. Spoon into greased 9" x 13" pan. Bake until browned, about one hour.

NO STARCH PASSOVER
APPLE AND NUT KUGEL (P)

```
2    large tart apples, pared and sliced
5    eggs, separated
1    cup chopped walnuts
1/4  cup honey
1/2  teaspoon salt
2    tablespoons sugar
1    tablespoon lemon juice
1    tablespoon grated lemon rind
```

Preheat oven to 350 degrees.   9 servings

Line bottom of greased 9" square pan with apple slices. Beat egg yolks until light and frothy. Add nuts, honey, salt, sugar, juice and rind. Blend well. Beat egg whites until stiff, not dry. Fold into mixture. Pour over apple slices. Bake 30 minutes or until set.

PINEAPPLE UPSIDE-DOWN MATZAH KUGEL (M) ✡

```
5    egg matzahs, broken into small pieces
3/4  cup brown sugar (divided, 1/2 cup and 1/4 cup)
8    slices canned pineapple in own juice, drained
6    large eggs
1/4  cup milk              1/2 cup raisins
1/2  cup butter            3   tablespoons lemon juice
1/2  teaspoon salt         2   teaspoons lemon peel, grated
1/2  teaspoon cinnamon     1/2 cup chopped nuts
1/4  teaspoon ginger       1/2 cup chopped dry fruit
```

Preheat oven to 350 degrees.   9 servings

Combine 3 beaten eggs with milk. Soak matzah pieces in mixture. Melt 1/4 cup butter in oven in bottom of 9" x 9" pan. Remove from oven and sprinkle with 1/4 cup brown sugar. Place pineapple slices on top. Beat the other 3 eggs and add remaining melted butter, remaining 1/2 cup brown sugar, salt, cinnamon, ginger, lemon juice and peel. Beat thoroughly. Add nuts and matzah mixture and fold in dried fruit and raisins. Pour into pan and bake 50 minutes, until set and golden brown. Let sit five minutes. Loosen edges and invert over serving dish.

MATZAH FARFEL AND WINE KUGEL (P)

```
3    cups matzah farfel or broken up matzah
3    eggs, separated
2/3  cups sugar
1/4  cups sweet red wine
1    teaspoon salt
3    tablespoons Passover oil
2    teaspoons orange rind, grated
```

Preheat oven to 350 degrees.   8 servings

Soak farfel or matzah in cold water, then drain. Beat yolks with sugar and add wine, salt, orange rind and oil. Mix into farfel. Fold stiffly beaten egg whites into mixture. Pour into greased 8" pan and bake 30 minutes.

PASSOVER FRUIT MEDLEY KUGEL (M)

4	cups matzah farfel
2	16 oz. cans sliced peaches, drained and cubed
1	cup pitted dates, diced
1/4	lb. plus 2 tablespoons Passover margarine, melted
8	large eggs
1/2	teaspoon ground nutmeg
1/2	cup plus 1 tablespoon sugar
8	ounces plain yogurt
8	ounces cottage cheeese with pineapple
1/2	cup walnuts, chopped
1/4	teaspoon ground cinnamon

Preheat oven to 350 degrees   16 Servings

Reserve 1/4 cup matzah farfel, 1/2 cup peaches and 1/4 cup dates for topping. In large bowl, combine remaining farfel and 1-1/2 cups warm water; set aside. Combine 1/4 lb. margarine, eggs, nutmeg and sugar. Add yogurt, cottage cheese and remaining peaches and dates. Fold in soaked farfel until blended. Pour mixture into greased 9" x 13" baking pan. Top with reserved peaches and dates. Combine remaining 2 tablespoons of margarine, chopped walnuts, cinnamon, 1 tablespoon sugar and reserved matzah farfel. Sprinkle mixture evenly over kugel. Bake 40 to 45 minutes until kugel is slightly puffed and set.

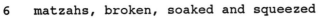

MATZAH KUGEL WITH WHITE WINE SAUCE (P)

6	matzahs, broken, soaked and squeezed
6	eggs, separated
1/2	cup sugar
2	teaspoons vanilla extract
1	teaspoon grated lemon peel
1	tablespoon lemon juice
4	tart apples, peeled and cubed
1/2	cup dark raisins
1/2	cup white raisins
1	cup sliced almonds
4	tablespoons pareve Passover margarine

Preheat oven to 350 degrees.   10 servings

Grease a 10" pan. Break matzahs into small pieces and soak in water until soft, drain and squeeze. Beat yolks about five minutes. Add sugar, vanilla, lemon peel, and lemon juice and mix thoroughly. Add, matzah, apples, raisins, and almonds. Beat egg whites until stiff. Fold in whites and pour into casserole dish. Dot with butter. Bake about 50 minutes until browned.

WHITE WINE SAUCE (P)

```
6    egg yolks (whites can be frozen)
3/4  cup sugar
1    cup kosher for Passover dry white wine
2    teaspoons potato starch
```

In a saucepan on top of a double boiler, slowly add sugar to beaten yolks. Gradually add wine and potato starch. Place over boiling water, stirring continuously until mixture begins to thicken (about 10 minutes). Serve hot or cold. Can refrigerate for 24 hours.

Carrots are probably the most popular vegetable used in Jewish homes during the holidays. Because the Yiddish word "mehren" can mean either "carrots" or "increase", carrots represent the desire that our virtues will be increased. When cut into thin, round slices, carrots look like gold coins. They symbolize increase in numbers and wealth.

CARROT PUDDING (P)

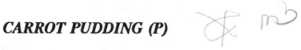

```
1    cup matzah meal
1/2  cup brown sugar
1    teaspoon salt
1    teaspoon baking soda*
1/2  cup oil
3    eggs, separated
3    cups grated raw carrots
```

Preheat oven to 350 degrees.   8 servings

Sift together dry ingredients; cream sugar and shortening. Beat egg yolks until light. Add egg yolks and dry ingredients alternately to creamed mixture and mix well. Stir in carrots and fold in stiffly beaten egg whites. Bake in well greased 8 " pan 40 minutes.

Note: Baking soda is a pure product and not a leavening agent and can be used for Passover!

PASSOVER CARROT KUGEL (P)

1/8 cup matzah meal
2   cups raw carrots, grated (tightly packed)
8   eggs, separated
1/2 cup potato starch
4   tablespoons lemon juice
4   teaspoons lemon peel, grated
1   cup sugar
1/2 cup wine (sweet red)
1/2 cup apple, shredded
1/2 cup chopped walnuts (optional)

Preheat oven to 375 degrees.   15 servings

Beat egg yolks with sugar until light. Add carrots,
apple, wine, lemon juice, lemon peel, matzah meal and
potato starch and mix thoroughly. Beat egg whites until
stiff and fold into carrot mixture. Spoon into 9" x 13"
pan sprayed with non-stick baking spray and bake 35-40
minutes. Serve hot or cold.

NO EGG CARROT, SWEET POTATO
AND APPLE KUGEL (P)

1/4 cup margarine, melted
1   cup sweet potatoes grated, peeled
1   cup carrots grated, peeled
1   cup apples, grated, peeled
1/2 cup matzah meal
1/2 teaspoon cinnamon
1/2 teaspoon nutmeg
1/4 cup white sugar
1/4 cup brown sugar
1/2 cup water
2   tablespoons sweet wine

Preheat oven to 375 degrees.   8 servings

Combine ingredients and pour into lightly greased 8" x
8" pan. Bake 45 minutes. Serves 8.

DIET DAIRY MATZAH KUGEL (M)

3   matzahs
1   lb. dry or low-fat cottage cheese
4   egg whites
6   packs heat stable artificial sweetener
1   teaspoon cinnamon
1   cup skim milk
1   tablespoon Passover margarine

Preheat oven to 350 degrees.   4 servings   160 calories

Mix cottage cheese, egg whites, sugar and cinnamon together. Pour milk into 8" square pan and soak matzahs (each one separately) about two minutes. Set matzahs aside; save leftover milk. Clean baking pan and then mess it up again by greasing it with non-stick baking spray. Place one piece of matzah on bottom of pan. Pour half of cheese mixture over it. Repeat the layering with another matzah and the rest of the cheese mixture. Top with third matzah. Dot with pieces of margarine. Cover everything with the saved milk. Bake uncovered 35-40 minutes or until concoction is set and golden.

NOT SWEET PASSOVER KUGEL

Also See: *Beautiful Zucchini Kugel, p. 131*
              Eggplant Kugel, p. 66
              Favorite Potato Kugel, p. 141
              Layered Fish and Potato Kugel, p. 143
              Matzos Pudding, p. 53
              Milk Potato Kugel, p. 142
              Mock Potato Kugel, p. 128
              Tzibble Kugel, p. 134
              Ugly Zucchini Kugel, p. 131

PASSOVER SPINACH KUGEL (P)

2   packages frozen spinach, cooked and drained
1   cup onions, chopped
1/2   cup celery, chopped
1/2   cup fresh mushrooms, sliced
1-1/2   cups carrots, grated
3/4   cup matzah meal
1   tablespoon Passover margarine
3   eggs, beaten
salt and pepper to taste

Preheat oven to 350 degrees   8 servings

Saute onion, celery, mushrooms and carrots until tender.
Add spinach, eggs, matzah meal, salt and pepper. Pour
into greased 10" pan. Bake for 45 minutes.

DIET CARROT KUGEL (F)

1-1/2 cups matzah, crumbled
1   cup kosher for Passover chicken bouillon
1-1/2 cups grated carrots (tightly packed)
1   tablespoon Passover oil
3   eggs, beaten
1   tablespoon dry onion flakes
1/2   teaspoon salt
2   teaspoons minced parsley

Preheat oven to 325 degrees.   6 servings   75 calories

Combine matzah and chicken bouillon and add eggs. Saute
carrots in oil and sprinkle with salt, parsley and onion
flakes. Pour into 1-1/2 quart baking dish. Bake 50
minutes or until firm.

GROUND CHICKEN KUGEL (F)

3   cups matzah meal
8   eggs, well beaten
1/2   teaspoon salt
2   tablespoons schmaltz (see recipe) or oil
2   cups water (approximately)
2-1/2 cups ground chicken, cooked
grebenes and onions from rendering schmaltz

Preheat oven to 350 degrees.   10 servings

Combine eggs with salt and fat. Add matzah meal, alternating with water. Use enough water to make a paste-like consistency. Place in refrigerator for 1 hour. Grease a round 10" souffle casserole pan. Combine chicken and grebenes and onions. Starting with matzah mixture, alternate with layers of chicken. End with matzah mixture. Bake one hour or until puffy, browned and firm. Serve with chicken soup.

SCHMALTZ AND GREBENES (F)

Remove fat and fatty skin from chicken. For each cup of fat to be rendered, you will need 1/4 cup of sliced onions and 1 apple slice. Wash and drain fat and skin and cut into small pieces. Cook over low heat until fat is almost melted. Add onions and apple and cook until onions are browned. Cool and drain. Onions and pieces of skin (grebenes or cracklings) can be stored in refrigerator for use in *fleishig* kugel or other recipes.

MATZAH KUGEL WITH GREBENES (F)

6   matzahs, soaked until soft and drained
1   onion, diced
1/4 cup schmaltz
1/4 cup chopped grebenes
3   eggs, beaten
3   tablespoons sugar
1   teaspoon salt
pepper to taste

Preheat oven to 350 degrees.   6 servings

Brown onion in schmaltz and add to matzahs. Add the rest of the ingredients. Bake in well greased 1-1/2 quart casserole dish one hour until browned. Serves 6-8.

MATZAH KUGEL WITH LIVER (F)

4 matzahs, soaked and squeezed
4 eggs, beaten
salt and pepper
1 lb. liver, chicken or beef, broiled
2 onions, diced and fried
schmaltz, just a little

Preheat oven to 325 degrees.   6 servings

Combine matzahs and eggs. Chop liver and onions
together and moisten with a little schmaltz. Season
with salt and pepper. Grease an 8" baking pan. Layer
matzah mixture, the liver and onions and end with
matzah. Bake 30 minutes or until browned.

CHICKEN SOUP MATZAH KUGEL (F)

6   matzahs, rinse, broken
2   eggs, beaten
1   onion
1/2   cup celery
1/2   cup green pepper, diced
1/2   cup carrots, grated
4   tablespoons schmaltz or Passover oil
1/4   teaspoon salt
1/4   teaspoon pepper
1   teaspoon paprika
2   tablespoons parsley
2-1/2 cups kosher for Passover chicken soup

Preheat oven to 350 degrees.   8 servings

Rinse (do not soak) broken matzahs. Saute onion,
carrots, green pepper and celery in schmaltz or oil and
season with salt, pepper and parsley. Combine matzahs,
eggs, chicken soup and add vegetables. Pour mixture
into a greased 9" baking pan. Bake one hour.

ABBREVIATIONS

tsp.	= teaspoon	oz.	= ounce
Tbsp.	= tablespoon	lb.	= pound
c.	= cup	sm.	= small
pt.	= pint	med.	= medium
qt.	= quart	lg.	= large

EQUIVALENTS

Dash.........................a few shakes or
                            8 drops
Pinch........................amount that can be
                            taken between thumb
                            and finger
Some and a little is the same as a pinch or a dash

1 Tbsp.....................3		tsp.
1/8 cup or 1 ounce...........2		Tbsp.
1/4 cup......................4		Tbsp.
1/3 cup......................5		Tbsp. + 1 tsp.
1/2 cup......................8		Tbsp.
2/3 cup......................10		Tbsp. + 2 tsp.
3/4 cup......................12		Tbsp.
4 oz.......1/4 lb. dry....1/2		cup liquid
8 oz.......1/2 lb. dry......1		cup liquid
16 oz.........1 lb. dry......2		cups liquid
	1	pint
32 oz........2 lbs. dry.....4		cups liquid
	1	quart

FRUIT CANS AND CONTENTS

No. 1.................1 lb.................2 cups		
No. 2.................1 lb. 4 oz......2-1/2 cups		
No. 2-1/2.............1 lb. 12 oz......3-1/2 cups		

FOOD EQUIVALENTS AND
SUBSTITUTIONS

Also see: *Sugar Substitutions, p. 27*
Cholesterol Watchers' Tips, p. 25

```
Apples...............1 lb...............3 medium or
                                        3 cups sliced
                     4 cups sliced......4 medium
Butter/margarine....1 stick............1/2 cup; 1/4 lb.
                                        8 Tbsp.
Carrots.............3 or 4.............3 cups
Corn flakes.........3 c. dry whole.....1 cup dry,crushed
Cottage Cheese......1/2 lb.............1 cup; 8 oz.
Cream Cheese........3 oz...............6 tablespoons
Eggs, whole.........1 cup.............5 large eggs
                    1 lb..............9 medium eggs
                    1 egg.............2 egg whites
       yolks...........1 cup............12 large yolks
       whites.........1 cup.............9 large whites
                    2 whites..........1 whole egg
       egg substitute..1 portion..........1 egg
Flour, all purpose..1 lb..............4 cups
                    1 oz..............4 tablespoons
                    1 cup sifted......1 cup instant
                                      1 cup + 2 Tbsp.
                                      cake flour
```

Passover substitutions for flour:

```
                     1 cup.............1/4 c.  matzah
                                       meal
                                       3/4 cup potato
                                       starch
                     1/2 cup...........2 Tbsp. matzah
                                       meal
                                       6 Tbsp. potato
                                       starch
Garlic..............1 med. clove......1/8 tsp. powder
Herbs, fresh........1 Tbsp.............1 tsp. dried
Lemon...............1 medium..........3 Tbsp. juice;
                                      1 Tbsp. rind
```

```
Milk, whole..........1 cup...........1/2 cup evapor-
                                      ated  milk  &
                                      1/2 cup water
      buttermilk.....1 cup............1 cup sweet milk
                                      plus 1  Tbsp.
                                      vinegar    or
                                      lemon   juice
Noodles..............1 lb. raw........9 cups cooked
Nuts:
   Almonds, in shell..1 lb............1/4 lb. nutmeat
                                      about 1 cup
   Pecans, in shell...1 lb............2-1/4 cups
                                      4 cups nutmeat
   Walnuts, in shell..1 lb............2 cups
                                      3-1/2 c. nutmeat
Onions...............6 or 7...........2-1/2 cups diced
                     1 small fresh.....1 Tbsp. instant
                                      minced rehy-
                                      drated
Orange...............1 medium.........1/3 cup juice
                                      2 Tbsp. rind
Peaches..............2 lbs............2 cups sliced
                                      8 medium
Potatoes:
   White.............1 lb............3 medium
                                      2-1/3 cups sliced
   Sweet (yams).......1 lb............3 medium
                                      3 cups sliced
Potato flour.........1 cup............1 c. pot. starch
Raisins..............1 lb............3 cups
Rice.................1 cup raw........3 cups cooked
Salt.................1 teaspoon.......1 teaspoon light
                                      salt
Schmaltz.............1 cup............1 cup oil
Sour cream...........1 cup............1/3 cup butter
                                      plus 2/3 cup
                                      buttermilk
Strawberries.........1 pint...........2 cups sliced
Sugar, white.........1 lb............2-1/4 cups
                     1 cup............1 c.firm packed
Vanilla extract......1 teaspoon.......1 Tbsp.imitation
                                      vanilla
                                      flavoring
```

GLOSSARY

DEFINITIONS OF COOKING TERMS

Al dente: Pasta or vegetables that are cooked slightly underdone. See parboiling.

Bake: To cook food by dry heat, usually in an oven

Baste: To moisten baked or roasted foods with liquid during baking.

Beating: Mixing or combining with a brisk, or rotary motion

Blanching: Submerging or dipping in boiling water and then plunging into cold water

Blend: To combine by stirring or mixing to a smooth consistency

Boiling: Cooking in liquid at boiling temperature (212 degrees fahrenheit)

Brush: To spread a thin coating of liquid or semi-liquid over the top

Caramelize: To dissolve sugar and water slowly, then heating until it thickens and turns caramel brown

Chopping: Cutting into very small pieces with a knife or food chopper

Combine: To mix or blend ingredients

Cracklings: The crisp brown pieces that remain when all the fat is rendered from poultry; grebenes

Creaming:	Stirring or mixing to a smooth and creamy softness
Cubing:	Cutting into cubes
Cutting in:	Distributing a creamy mixture through a dry mixture by aid of a cutting motion with a knife, spatula or pastry blender
Dash:	A small quantity; several quick shakes of a spice shaker
Dice:	To cut into very small pieces about 1/2 inch in size
Dissolve:	To blend together a liquid and solid substance
Dotting:	Scattering small bits over the surface
Dough:	A mixture of ingredients including flour and liquid, blended or kneaded smooth enough to form into desired shapes by rolling or patting
Drain:	To remove liquid from solids by pouring through a colander or sieve
Drizzle:	To slowly pour a very thin stream of liquid lightly over food
Dusting:	Sprinkling lightly over surface with dry, powdery ingredients such as sugar, spices and flour
Fleishig:	Meat or its derivatives, or combinations containing same. Dishes and utensils so designated
Flouring:	Dusting or rolling in flour
Folding in:	To combine ingredients with a gentle stroke of spoon or fork downward through the mixture, along bottom of container then upwards until blended and air is incorporated
Grating:	Reducing to fine particles, usually with a grater or food processor
Grease:	To lightly coat a pan with some fat to prevent foods from sticking and to help browning

Grebenes:	See cracklings
Kashruth:	Regulations taken from Jewish law codes pertaining to food and daily life
Knead:	To work into a smooth and elastic mass by pressure of the hand, using the heel of the thumb
Latkes:	Pancakes that are usually deep fried
Leaven:	To cause a mixture to rise while it is baking by adding baking powder, baking soda or yeast
Melt:	To heat until liquid and pourable
Milchig:	Milk derivatives. Foods containing no meat derivative. Dishes and utensils so designated
Mince:	To chop or cut up very fine
Mixing:	Combining ingredients until evenly distributed
Parboiling:	"Al dente." Cooking in boiling water until partially soft
Pare:	To remove outer covering from fruits and vegetables with a knife
Pareve:	Neutral - can be eaten with dairy or meat meals; containing no meat derivatives and no milk derivatives
Peel:	To strip off outer covering from fruits and vegetables; the outer skin or rind or a fruit or vegetable. Grated for some recipes
Pesahdic:	Prepared for the week of Passover. Approved for Passover use and marked accordingly
Pit:	To remove the pits from fruit
Plump:	To soak dried fruits in liquid until they swell and are rehydrated
Preheat:	To set oven at the desired temperature before use so that desired temperature is reached inside oven before food is

put in to cook. It usually takes 10 to 15 minutes in most ovens.

Render: To liquify solid fat over low heat

Rind: The outer skin or peel of a fruit or vegetable. Grated for some recipes

Saute: To cook until browned and tender in a small amount of fat in an uncovered pan

Schmaltz: Chicken or goose fat

Shredding: Cutting or tearing into thin pieces or strips, with the aid of a knife, grater or food processor

Sift: To pass dry ingredients, usually flour, through a fine-mesh strainer to remove lumps and lighten texture

Simmer: To cook liquid alone or along with other ingredients over low heat. Some small bubbles will usually appear on the surface

Souffle: A baked food, either a dessert or entree made light and fluffy by the addition of beaten egg whites before cooking

Steam: To cook food, covered over a small amount of boiling water

Stir: To blend a mixture together using a spoon in a circular motion

Stock: Broth made from meat, poultry, fish or vegetables with the addition of herbs and spices

Whipping: Using a brisk, rotary motion to allow air into mixture of ingredients. Beating eggs, cream or combinations of both with fork or rotary beater.

INDEX

mmmm yum!